T0196007

A Family's Journey Through Autism

Maggie Weathersby

authorHOUSE®

AuthorHouse™
1663 Liberty Drive
Bloomington, IN 47403
www.authorhouse.com
Phone: 1 (800) 839-8640

Published by AuthorHouse 01/09/2020

ISBN: 978-1-7283-4181-1 (sc)
ISBN: 978-1-7283-4179-8 (hc)
ISBN: 978-1-7283-4180-4 (e)

Library of Congress Control Number: 2020900309

Print information available on the last page.

"This family's journey will keep you turning the pages…very heartwarming, inspiring and truly incredible!"

— Cathy K.

***

"I thought the book was insightful and filled with raw emotion. It made me laugh, cry and thankful all at the same time. Sharing feelings many of us could not put into word as we struggle through personal difficulties in our lives it made me feel I wasn't alone and gives hope that we can overcome as long as we have faith in God he will get us through it."

— Cathy S.

Hardship often prepares an ordinary person for an extra ordinary destiny.

—C. S. Lewis

"I held her! I told her everything would be all right, and I held her! Oh my God! What have I done to my little girl?"

I had replayed the moments in the doctor's office that day a million times in my mind throughout the weeks that followed, dissecting each word and action frame by frame, all the while praying desperately in the quietness of my heart that it would somehow change the outcome. Yet, things remained as they were.

The unusual combination for disaster that day included a fourteen-month-old child, a doctor's visit, and a nurse. Not in my wildest dreams had I imagined that a simple routine visit had the potential to virtually alter our path as a family.

My questions were as numerous as the stars, and a reasonable explanation was literally nonexistent. What do I do? Where do I go? Who do I talk to? And even more perplexing, *what* just happened?

I remember being on my knees for weeks after it all happened, adamantly begging God to somehow help me go back in time and reverse that day, but it seemed as though my prayers were intercepted before they even reached heaven's doors. As my own personal nightmare began to evolve, I suddenly understood how Daniel (in the Bible) must have felt when he went from being the king's number one man to being hurled into the lion's den without hardly a warning.

I understand that God's deliverance methods are far from what we envision, but would it be asking too much of fate for Him to simply step in and help me this time?

My plan was for God to somehow magically reverse things so I could continue in my happy little world as though nothing had happened. *But*

God's plan was for me to trust Him, no matter what I saw and no matter what I heard—just trust! Jeremiah 29:11 says: *"For I know the plans I have for you, declares the Lord, plans to prosper you and not to harm you, plans to give you a hope and a future"*.

The journey to success isn't always a glamourous one. It is, however, worth it if you are willing to stay the course! So, I invite you to walk with me through the incredible pain, guilt, and unbelievable miracles that could only come from trusting an *amazing God*! In our *Family's Journey through Autism!*

CHAPTER 1

THE VISIT

"I'm taking Dani for her shots later today, so dinner might be a bit late." Those were the last words I exchanged with my husband as he was leaving for work on June 5, 1996. It was a nice sunny day, and I was happy that I could start taking walks with the girls again. It appeared as though the winter had taken its toll on them, as well as me. Danielle, was a joyful little cutie with strawberry-blonde curls that danced on her head and hazel eyes that she would have to grow into at some point. Danielle Ann had entered this world weighing eight pounds, two ounces just fourteen months earlier on March 15, 1995, three hours and nine minutes after labor began.

The delivery was without incident, but an amazing thing happened as she was tossed on my belly. As we were momentarily looking eye to eye, I felt a surge of unbelievable intuition go through me, so intense that it was as if someone said out loud, "This is not going to be easy!" I even looked around to see whether anyone else had heard it. I didn't realize at the time that it was the motherly instinct that God graciously bestows upon all mommies. So, feeling a bit embarrassed, I quickly shook it off and softly gathered my precious little angel in my arms before they whisked her away to do all the little tests for newborns. Two days later, when we brought Danielle home as the newest addition to our family, Ashley delightfully greeted us at the door with Grandma to catch the first glimpse of her little sister. Ashley was a beautiful blonde-haired cutie who at the age of two had already figured out that the world belonged to her—and if she had to spend the rest of her life proving it, well, so be it. She was an incredibly bright and caring child whose heart made up the biggest part of who she was.

Everything was normal as we arrived at the doctor's office. Danielle weighed eighteen pounds, five ounces, and her height was twenty-nine and a quarter inch. In all, she looked great and was given a very healthy checkup. The doctor looked at her chart and said that her exam looked great and that the nurse would be right in to give Danielle her shots. This is the part that I think every parent dislikes, but as we all know, vaccinations are so very important for our children. As the nurse walked in, I began to prepare Dani for the shot and held her close to me, reassuring her that everything would be all right. But right at the end of the injection, when the syringe was fully extended, Danielle jerked her arm so quickly that the needle came out.

The nurse immediately turned to me, exclaiming, "Ooh!" I asked what was wrong, and she explained, rather upset, that the needle had come out and so had the vaccine. I said that I didn't see it squirt out but observed only a simple beadlike drop on Danielle's arm. The nurse maintained that all the vaccine had come out and would have to be administered again.

I was convinced the vaccine had remained in my daughter, so I adamantly pressed the nurse as to why she felt a second shot was necessary. The nurse, who had already begun to make her way toward the door, swung around and with absolute authority stated that she would, in fact, give the shot again. Because by law, she coldly added, if it wasn't recorded in her medical records as being administered, then it would be as if Danielle had never had it. She reiterated that the vaccine did squirt out of her arm, and she would not record it if I didn't allow her to administer it again. With that, she abruptly left the room.

How does a parent describe the feeling of knowing that what is about to take place is beyond wrong? I felt greatly intimidated by how quick she was to use the law as her defense. As she reentered the room, I felt a coldness from her that went clear through me. I tried once more to reason with her and strongly suggested that the doctor be asked to come into the room before she went any further. She simply said no, grabbed Danielle's arm, and instantly injected her with the vaccine a second time. It took Danielle more than five seconds to cry from the unexpected poke, and the same amount for my heart to start beating again. We both were incredibly stunned.

All she said was, "Now there. That wasn't so bad, was it?"

I believe with all my heart that there is a price to pay when people push their arrogance on innocent people. I left the doctor's office haunted by the fact that I didn't just get up and walk out of the room or at the least insist more adamantly that the doctor be brought in. Yet to be realistic, I don't believe that I could have anticipated her actions. As I was walking out of the office that day, I remember thinking that I always assumed that doctors' offices were supposed to be kind and professional when dealing with families. That was definitely not the case that day.

For the next couple of days, Danielle seemed cranky but after that seemed calmer for the most part. I was still upset about what took place in the doctor's office with the nurse, but I managed to push it aside and go on with what was left of the week.

June 11, 1996, started out like any other day. Ashley had awoken early and was sitting on the couch, giggling and enjoying her favorite show, *Barney*. I briefly stopped in to kiss her good morning and proceeded to the kitchen to prepare a bottle for Danielle, whom I could hear chattering away through the monitor on the counter. As I walked up the steps to Danielle's bedroom, I hesitated at the doorway. "Good morning, my love," I said. Then I noticed a red mark on the side of her right cheek. As I approached her crib, I made some playful talk about there being a bug in her bed. I kept rambling away in my mommy talk, glancing around her crib to see if I could find anything, but after a moment, I laid her down to change her while she contentedly drank her bottle.

But when I unsnapped her pajamas and pulled her legs from the pant legs, I was stunned to discover that both legs seemed to be covered in bug bites as well. I looked around her crib, saying, "That bug is really in trouble now!" But after coming up empty-handed again, I went back to changing her, now more cautiously.

As I slowly removed the rest of the pajamas and then her T-shirt, there are no words to describe what I felt. It was one of those moments that leave you breathless and paralyzed with fear. My mind was saying, *Wow, I've never seen so many bug bites before*, but my soul was saying, *this is bad!* I wanted to believe my mind over my soul, yet it only took a second to realize that these were *not* bug bites. I don't know when my heart started to beat again, but my instincts said, *Get her to the doctor!* I grabbed her up in my arms, the tears already stinging on my face, and bolted down the steps. As I reached for the phone to call the doctor's office, I saw my hand shaking uncontrollably. My efforts to be calm were failing miserably. I could hear my husband asking what was wrong, but my anxiety seemed to be in charge, and I couldn't reply.

After three tries, I finally dialed the correct number. When the receptionist answered, I told her that my daughter had what looked like bug bites all over her body, and I wanted to bring her in right away. The receptionist said she would check to see if there was an available time.

In sheer panic, I interrupted. "I'm sorry, but I wasn't asking for an appointment. I'm telling you that I'm getting ready, and when I am, I'm coming in! Something is wrong … Please, just look at her." I began to apologize and cry at the same time.

The receptionist, knowing what anxiety can do to a parent, calmly said, "It's going to be okay, Maggie. Just bring her in, and the doctor will see her when you arrive."

By the time I hung up the phone, my husband had made his way to my side, and I began to explain what was happening to our child. We looked her over and discovered no fewer than eighty to a hundred of these apparent bug bites on her little body. On the way to the doctor's office, I tried to tell myself that everything was okay—this was just some strange rash that would go away in a few days. That worked until I picked her up from the car seat only to discover that the little red bites had merged together so rapidly that they were now huge welts all over her. A couple were the size of golf balls in circumference. Her outer ears were so swollen that she looked like she had Dumbo ears, and there was so much swelling under her armpits that they looked like breasts. She was quite the sight.

Upon arriving at the doctor's office, we were taken right into be seen by our pediatrician's associate who after a couple minutes of, "Hmmmm, okay, yes," announced that it was a good case of hives. I asked how one goes about getting hives since I was unfamiliar with them. She matter-of-factly explained to me that I must have given Danielle something different in her diet, and this was her body's way of reacting to it. I was pretty sure that I hadn't given her anything out of the ordinary and expressed this to the doctor, but after a brief discussion on the matter, she told me to give Danielle some Benadryl to stop the itching, and in a couple of days it should all be cleared up. I felt momentarily satisfied, as did my husband, but truth be known, my heart wasn't so easily soothed. I kept a constant eye on her that day and was up most of the night watching her, for fear something else might happen, and I wouldn't catch it in time. I was learning firsthand that the word *mom* entailed much more than just giving birth.

The next day I was exhausted from lying awake thinking about everything all night, so I forced myself to believe it was hives as the doctor had said and went on with my day. It was my husband's birthday; the sun was out, and we were going to have fun no matter what. So, pushing everything aside, I busied myself with the day, going to the market, cleaning, cooking, and having a birthday party fit for a terrific daddy. It was somewhere between the hours of two and four o'clock in the afternoon. The cake was made, the children were bathed, dinner was ready, and I decided to cut out some last-minute decorations to hang on the wall. As I sat down on the television room floor to finish up the last of the decorations, Danielle (who had been standing next to me) passed by to go into the playroom. As she did, I caught a glimpse of her and was instantly mortified from the inside out! All the welts and red marks from the previous day that we were told were hives seemed to be replaced by bruises. I had a wave of nausea pass through me so strong that I could hardly move but pushed past it and immediately began looking her over as I had the day before. I discovered that all the previous hives were replaced by these enormous bruises that literally encompassed no less than three-quarters of her body. She looked as though she had either been beaten or hit by a car. The only words that managed to quietly escape from me were, "Oh my God, my baby!"

Everything seemed to move in slow motion for the next couple of minutes. I carefully scooped her up in my arms and held her close to me as the tears streamed down my face in silent fear. I quietly went to the phone and called the doctor's office and asked to be connected to a nurse on call.

After a short moment, the nurse answered, and I simply said, "I don't know much about hives, but do they turn to bruises before they go away?"

There was a piercing silence that shot through me. After what seemed like an eternity, the nurse finally spoke up and said, "Take Danielle to the medical center, Maggie, and the doctor will meet you there."

After I hung up, I held Danielle close and whispered a prayer so intense that I'm sure every angel in heaven heard it and cried with me.

CHAPTER 2

HAPPY BIRTHDAY?

Trying hard not to let panic overtake me, I called my husband, who was just about to leave work, and told him what had happened and asked that he please meet us at the medical center. The ride over was calm and eerie. The only one who seemed to not be affected by it all was Ashley. As I drove, I could hear her chattering away, singing to herself and occasionally looking up at me for my approval. It was actually quite soothing to listen to her rather than the thoughts that were going through my mind. I knew that whatever this was, it wasn't going to be a good thing, and I just wanted it to be over with and everything to be back the way it was before. As we entered the medical center parking lot, I spotted my husband's car and felt a moment of relief. I wanted to run up to him and cry, but I knew if I allowed myself to get emotional, I wouldn't be able to go through with the office visit. I felt that my daughter needed me to be strong for her more than ever that night. As we neared the entrance, I had this overwhelming urge to turn and run as fast as I could but instead kept walking.

Once inside the medical center, everything kind of happened rather quickly. We signed in and were immediately taken into a room where our pediatrician looked her over carefully and said that he wanted to have blood work done to check her white blood count. I probingly asked him what he was looking for, and he said they were looking for leukemia or whatever else they could possibly detect. He also requested that I be patient, and when the tests came back, they would be explained to us as we went along. He then stated that he was confident things would most likely come back okay. Most likely, that meant that there was a chance it could be something fatal. (Isn't that just like human nature to always think of the worst scenario before giving God the opportunity to show us how awesome He really is?) I felt as if my mind had separated itself from reality, and the words kept echoing throughout my head. Why couldn't this be a week ago when she was playing and laughing, and everything was happy in her world? Not this daunting feeling that just kept traveling between my heart and mind. What happened that put us here tonight? Where was the laughter?

My mind was suddenly flooded by a barrage of questions, each one more frightening than the last. I was rescued from my thoughts when the doctor said, "Excuse me," as if I were in the next room. As I slid back into reality, I was aware that nothing had changed. We were still in the room with the doctor and my little Danielle was still covered with the same horrible bruises I'd discovered just a few hours before. As we went to the lab to have her blood drawn, my husband informed me that I would have to go in with her because he didn't do needles. So, he agreed to stay in the waiting room with our oldest child, Ashley, who still thought it was a great idea to go the doctor's office and play with all his toys instead of hers. Upon sitting in the chair, Danielle on my lap facing forward, I felt the silent fear that had been lingering in my mind since the doctor's visit the week before still trying to have its way, so I held my arms tightly but gently around my little girl so as not to lose my grip. My eyes watered as I softly sang, "Jesus loves me, this I know." The more she screamed, the louder I sang. "For the Bible tells me so."

After a moment, I realized that the nurses had joined in too. "Little ones to him belong. They are weak, but He is strong."

As the second vial was being filled, one nurse finished the song as the tears and my heart had finally gotten the better of me. When everything was over, they passed out the tissues, and we went off to the waiting room to await the results.

After about fifteen or twenty minutes, I spotted a gentleman who resembled what I viewed as the medical technician moving rather quickly from the lab. (His white coat was pretty much a giveaway.) He seemed very engrossed in the folder he was reading as he passed through the waiting room, and almost instinctively, I jumped up and caught his attention.

I cautiously but abruptly said, "Excuse me." And as he turned around, I uttered, "I'm sorry to bother you, but my husband and I are waiting for some blood work taken in the lab for our daughter, and I was wondering if the folder you're holding would be them?"

His reply was, "And you are?"

"I'm Maggie, her mom."

"And your daughter's name?"

"Danielle," I stated with a warm grin.

"Hmm … Yes, well it states here that your daughter's white blood count is quite high, but that's about all I'm at liberty to say at this time. If you'll have a seat, your pediatrician will be right with you and clear up any questions you and your husband might have. Okay?" He then vanished as quickly as he appeared.

The white blood count being off didn't sound too good but, I wanted to hear what the doctor had to say before I worked myself into a panic. At that moment, the nurse who a week before had given my daughter two helpings of the MMR (measles, mumps, and rubella) vaccine was on duty and made her way over to us. She knelt down to Danielle and talked to her as if she were hers by birth. I had the sudden urge to tell her to get away from her but decided to keep my feelings to myself and quietly asked God to help me forgive her.

Truth was, there were more important things to concentrate on at the moment. Shortly after they called our names, we were escorted into a big room. I immediately went toward the window with the warm sunshine.

I could sense we were about to be told something bad, and I wanted to be as close to the happiest thing I could find, even if it was just the sun. There were two doctors who walked into the room. The first was our regular pediatrician, and the other I had never seen before. Greetings were extended, and our doctor began to speak. I could tell from his proper handling of words and the way he carefully read the huge book that lay in front of him that he wanted to go on record as saying the right things. I quietly listened to what he read and then to the explanation of it so that we could understand the full impact of what this was going to mean for our little girl as well as our family.

He said Danielle had what was called Henoch-Schoenlein syndrome purpura. It's a type of hypersensitivity vasculitis and inflammatory response within the blood vessel. It is caused by an abnormal response of the immune system. The exact cause for this disorder is unknown, but the incidence in boys is greater than girls. The syndrome is usually seen in children, but people of any age may be affected. The symptoms usually resolve within one week, but they may reappear several times before complete remission. In short, as he summed it up for us, Danielle was in no danger of dying, but (worst-case scenario) there was a chance that she could hemorrhage into her kidneys, which would give her permanent kidney damage and cause her to require dialysis treatments.

Wow! What do you say to that? My husband and I both stood there quite stunned and amazed that this was even happening

I immediately asked, "So how does a person go about getting this?"

His reply was simply "I don't really know. This kind of thing is basically more of a mystery, and I believe your daughter could be the youngest one to have had it."

That wasn't exactly the answer I had in mind. "What do you mean you don't know?" I blurted out. "I mean, it's not like she was over Johnny's house last week, and—oh my gosh—he had Henoch-Schönlein syndrome purpura, so of course she caught it. My God! Work with me here!"

My voice had risen quite a bit since I'd begun speaking, and the doctor spoke up and asked me to please compose myself. So, after a short pause, I began (in a much calmer voice) to tell him my observations.

"A week ago, I brought a beautiful, healthy child to your office for a wellness checkup, and now you're telling me that there is a possibility that she could have permanent kidney damage? This is not something that you just wake up with one morning. This is more like a ... reaction to something!" And as I said it, I remembered the double shot of the MMR that was given to her and felt like an explosion went off in my head. "Oh my gosh! That's it!" I exclaimed. "The nurse insisted on giving Danielle another MMR shot again after I argued that it hadn't squirted out of her arm."

I then went through the whole scenario with the doctor, explaining in detail what had taken place in the office almost a week prior between the nurse and me. Then something else dawned on me that shook me to the core. "I held her! I told her that everything would be all right, and I held her. Oh my God! What did I do to my little girl?"

As I was in the process of verbally beating myself up, the doctor spoke up and said, "Now we can't go jumping to conclusions."

I felt irate and betrayed all in the same moment. Taking cautious steps toward both doctors, I firmly stated, "Well then, what can we conclude? That Danielle one day just woke up with all this stuff on her body? Excuse me, but I don't know of any person in their right mind who would believe a line of baloney like that!"

Our doctor stood up and said, "You can't medically prove it was because of the shots, Mrs. Weathersby!"

To which I replied, "*Really?* Well you can't medically prove it wasn't, *Doctor!*"

We all stood there in a somber silence. Our bodies had unconsciously positioned themselves in a north versus south stance for a moment before the doctor broke the tense silence and exclaimed, "Well whatever the cause,

I think we need to concentrate on getting Danielle through this before we go pointing fingers."

He was right. There was no proof as to the exact cause, and the bottom line was that we still needed to get Danielle through this, regardless of what caused it. The most critical period would be the next week, and it would be less critical every week after that. In a nutshell, we were told to keep a very close eye on her for the next year because anything could happen.

Our pediatrician told us that there was no reason to put her in the hospital because there was nothing they could watch for any more than we could at home and that she would be more comfortable in her own surroundings. The drive home was very quiet, and I just kept going over and over the doctor's visit the week before in my mind. I had this horrible sick feeling in the pit of my stomach because I had held her for the shots. Why didn't I protest more? Why didn't I know more about the vaccines that were being injected into my child's body? I was blaming myself for everything. By the time we arrived home I was numb with pain for my little girl from the inside out. As we all stepped into the house, I suddenly remembered that it was my husband's birthday, and all the preparations done earlier to make it a wonderful day suddenly felt in vain. As I looked at my husband's face, I sensed a strange distance that I had never seen in him before.

We went through the motions of singing "Happy Birthday," and he went through the motion of saying thank you. It was more than obvious that neither one of us was in a celebrating mood. After the girls had eaten their cake, I gently cleaned them up and scooted them off to the playroom so my husband and I could talk. As I stood across the counter, I looked into his eyes and could immediately sense that he was not handling the news well.

I decided to offer up some conversation and said, "So what are we going to do?"

His reply was short but devastating. He simply looked at me and said, "No, what are *you* going to do? I have to go to work!" With that, he walked into the playroom, kissed the girl's good night, and went upstairs to bed. I stood there frozen in unbelief. I felt like he blamed me for everything, which made me blame myself even more. After I put the girls down for the night, I came downstairs and sat on the sofa in a thick silence that seemed to engulf my whole being. Had I endangered my little girl and at the same time lost my marriage over it? I was praying that this was some kind of silly nightmare and at any moment I would wake up and things would be as they were before. But the truth was this was reality. And the nightmare had just begun.

CHAPTER 3

UNTIMELY DENIAL

The next day brought no relief from the pain that had invaded our home. Halfway through the day our pediatrician called to check up on Danielle and see how she was doing. I told him that some of the bruises had faded only to be replaced by more in another area of her body. He told me this was all quite normal and that soon they would stop appearing altogether. To look at her broke your heart, but she truly seemed not to notice except for an occasional scratch and whimper.

She was remarkable throughout the whole ordeal, which actually strengthened me. In speaking with the doctor, he stated that on the record he could not say one way or the other about what he personally felt might have caused such a reaction. Off the record, however, his guess would be that the MMR seemed to be the most likely culprit, yet nothing could be proven one way or the other. So, we came to the conclusion that we needed to focus on Danielle and not the cause for the time being. There would be opportunity enough in the future to discuss the cause and effects of it all, but now was not the time.

The next couple of weeks seemed to come and go with only a couple reappearing red marks followed by bruises. However, as the weeks went by and the marks disappeared, something strange emerged that was even more alarming than the marks.

Danielle seemed not to respond to her name anymore. If she looked your way, it was almost purely coincidental. I would call her ten different ways, and she would still act as if she had never heard me. This was combined with the fact that her verbal abilities were diminishing almost daily. When we were with other children her age, I would stand back and check her overall abilities compared to that of her peers, and she was beginning to fall very short in comparison. I also noticed that she was beginning to hide in, under, and behind things.

For example, we had a toy closet in our television room, and she would go in it, leaving only a crack open so that no one could see her, and she would watch television from there. Videos and movies were almost mesmerizing to her. I was amazed at how long she could stand there without moving and watch certain movies from beginning to end, yet she couldn't keep eye contact very well anymore. I remember sharing my observations with my husband and wanting so much for him to hold me and reassure me that everything would be all right, but he seemed so distant and preoccupied. Sometimes it seemed as if he did not care at all.

Why won't he talk to me? I would ask God at night when I fell on my knees. What I didn't know, however, was that my husband was in denial, and things were about to get much worse. Within a few short months, Danielle had gotten to the point that she would scream uncontrollably when my husband came in from work at night. In turn, he started to work later so that he would come home only after the children were asleep. I didn't know what to say or do, but my prayers were that God would take this awful thing away from my precious little girl! Yet, it was the kind of thing that left me totally confused and defenseless as to what was going on, let alone what I should do.

By November 1996, at twenty months old, our little Danielle was like a little deaf child who would walk through the house as if she were the only one in it. My parents came for Thanksgiving that year, and it was even obvious to them that something was not right. A private phone call from my mom confirmed my feelings shortly after they left. I was overwhelmed with the frustration of it all. I knew something was horribly wrong with our little girl, yet every time the conversation came up, my husband would simply say, "She's fine. Don't try and make something out of nothing!" He would then walk away and busy himself with some project around the house to avoid further discussion.

At Christmastime that year, I recall the living room being so full of toys that it looked like Santa had dropped off the whole toy store instead of just my girls' portion. Yet, as Ashley lost herself in the middle of the room, Danielle acted as if nothing were in sight with the exception of an eighty-nine-cent pull toy that stimulated her repeatedly. Again, I felt an incredible urgency sweep through me as though I needed to do something. *But what? I ask myself. What?*

By Danielle's second birthday, she had lost almost all her eye contact and verbal abilities. Her hands flapped uncontrollably when she was anxious or excited, and as if that weren't enough, another bizarre twist started to emerge. Every time her hands would flap from being excited or stimulated, her eyes would simultaneously roll up in her head almost to the point of not being able to see anything but the whites. The first time I saw her do it I thought she was going into convulsions, but then it happened more and more throughout the day as it became a part of the sick ritual that had seemingly encompassed our child. It was the thing that could most unnerve me in an instant.

Just days before her second birthday I took her for her wellness checkup, and after a few minutes of observing her, our pediatrician sat quietly on the chair in front of me and said, "Does she respond to anything?"

That was all it took—just five simple words—and I began to release a year's worth of fear and anxiety right there in his office. All those months of watching, observing, and wondering if I were really seeing what I was seeing came to a very realistic climax. The pediatrician and I spent the next thirty to forty minutes discussing what steps to take next. We would start by getting a hearing test, and whatever the results where, we would take it from there.

Tears were beginning to be no stranger to me. I cried silently to myself during the day and out loud on my knees to God at night after the kids were in bed. *Why should today be any different?* I thought to myself as I walked to the car feeling incredibly overwhelmed.

I wanted to sit down and talk to my husband but knew it would be out of the question. Things had gotten so bad between us that we weren't really speaking much anymore. And if we did speak, it would only turn into an argument. So, we basically said what was necessary and just kind of left it at that. Between Danielle's screaming for hours during the day and the strange rituals she had acquired and the angry outbursts from my husband at night, I was beginning to feel like I was losing my grip on reality. The only peace I felt was when I was on my knees talking to God or with my oldest child, Ashley. Together, those two things brought the sanity I needed to make it through one more day. Even then, I felt as though I was coming up on the short end of things.

That night, however, I tried to talk to my husband one more time about Danielle and what the doctor and I had discussed earlier that day in his office. Yet, it was to no avail. He kept changing the subject and cursed at me for whatever he could find that wasn't done to his liking as he looked around the house. I decided in that moment that I had endured all that I could. I believed that he loved us, but his own fears and frustrations were tearing us apart, not only as a couple but as a family. I felt like I was drowning, and I desperately needed to come up for air. The next morning, after he left for work, I loaded the children into our minivan and headed for my sister's house in Michigan.

The drive alone was a break from all that consumed me in the proceeding weeks. As I drove and the children slept, I was able to think more clearly than I had in months. I loved my husband and told him so in a letter I left, but something had to break. Either we worked on this problem together, or I would do it alone with God's help.

Every time I looked at my daughter and all the bizarre behaviors that had begun to envelop her, I felt this urgency shoot through me as if I were running out of time. We stayed in Michigan for about six weeks, and during that time, I was able to step back and evaluate things more clearly.

I remember how I cried openly one night as my sister lovingly shared her observations about Danielle. Although the reality of her words frightened me, they also allowed me to release the pain I had built up over the past year. They gave me a focal point to begin this journey we were about to embark on. God always knows who to put in your pathway and when to do it. By the time six weeks were up, my husband and I had begun talking on a regular basis, and I knew it was time to return and try to work this out together. So, in April 1997, my husband flew down to escort his family home, and we drove back to begin our journey together—or would we?

CHAPTER 4

HOMEWARD BOUND

The ride home was wonderful, and we talked and discussed things more than we ever had before. Danielle didn't seem to really notice her father, while Ashley talked a mile a minute to him about her adventures while visiting Auntie Marsha's house. The first couple of weeks went by very quickly because there was so much to do, and after speaking with our pediatrician, a referral was made to check Danielle's hearing.

On June 19, 1997, I took my little Danielle to the local medical center to the audiologist. The testing took about an hour, and all in all, she did quite well. After, we went into the administrator's office and sat down to discuss the results. Danielle started to flap her hands wildly and scream the same way she did when we were at home. I felt sick to my stomach and wanted to cry, but the hearing specialist was very warm and accepting of the moment and calmly told me it would be okay.

As I held Danielle in my arms, she quickly fell asleep, which allowed me to speak freely. I had quietly prayed in my heart before we entered the hospital that day that my daughter was indeed deaf, as horrible as it might have seemed. The alternative of not being deaf was much more horrifying to me as a mother. I expressed this to the audiologist, and she said she understood perfectly where I was coming from and not to be so hard on myself. We discussed what steps I would need to take next and where to take them. She said that Danielle needed to be evaluated for her language and speech delays, which were becoming a great concern.

So I was referred to the Child Development Center, located not too far from our home. I was feeling low when I left because I wanted so much for it all to end with her hearing. Little did I know, however, that this nightmare that had somehow befallen our little family was far from being over. When I got home that day, I put the girls to bed for a nap, made a nice hot cup of coffee, and sat down to gather my thoughts and focus on what to do next. Before I picked up the phone, I quietly bowed my head and asked God to guide my footsteps and to help the proper people to cross my path.

A quiet peace came over me as I dialed the number to the early intervention office. A wonderful woman whose name was Mandy happened to answer. Her voice was calm and inviting, which made it easy to talk to her. It turned out she was the director of the intervention center. As I began to talk about Danielle with her, I could tell she genuinely cared, which made it even more comforting to share about my daughter. After I explained our situation, she informed me that we would need to start with an assessment. This is where she would personally come to our home to meet my daughter and our family to get as much information as she could about her. At that point, she would let me know if an evaluation was needed. So, an appointment was scheduled, and we were on to the next step.

A couple of weeks later Mandy came to our home to meet Danielle and our family. After about an hour or so of speaking with her, she very kindly said that Danielle was a beautiful little girl and that it probably couldn't hurt to have her evaluated. I'm sure that in observing her that day it was not hard to see that there was a major problem going on. Yet she remained very professional and polite throughout the whole visit. The calm way she spoke helped me to feel more at ease, and to be honest, I actually looked forward to the evaluation scheduled for eleven o'clock the morning of July 22, 1997.

I was up early that day. The sun was shining, and I was feeling confident that maybe things would turn out better than I originally had expected. Who knew? Maybe I really was reading more into it than I should. I was trying desperately to convince myself that all was well with her, but I was only setting myself up for another emotional letdown. Just before we pulled up into the parking lot, I happened to glance in the rearview mirror only to see Danielle's hands flapping uncontrollably and her eyes rolled so far up in the sockets that it looked like they were stuck. As I parked the van, I quietly got out of my seat and put my hand gently on the side of her face as if to caress her and softly said, "Stop … please … stop!" I took her out of the car seat and, despite her protesting, held her in my arms anyway.

After we went inside, I found the office on the first floor just like Mandy had said. It was very welcoming—the kind of place that made you feel right at home. We were greeted by a very polite woman named Missy. (The secretary for early intervention.) After talking to Ashley and Danielle a moment, she told me to have a seat and someone would be right with us. We sat and within five minutes were greeted by Mandy who escorted us into a room where her associate Joni was waiting to help conduct the evaluation.

After the proper introductions were made, they busied Ashley with some toys and got right to business. They explained to me the various areas that they would be covering during the evaluation and asked that I not encourage Danielle to say or do anything because it could possibly hinder the outcome. So, I sat at the end of a child-sized table and watched them go to work on my little girl. They were quite impressive, to say the least. Ashley interrupted a couple of times, but Mandy gently redirected her and went right back to work. As I quietly watched them, it suddenly dawned on me that Danielle was failing miserably, and I had this overwhelming urge to jump in and help her but knew I couldn't. She was on her own this time, so I just sat there helplessly and watched as they did their best to get her to cooperate with them. At one point, there was a flashlight brought out (for what reason I don't remember), but she grabbed it, stuck it in her eye with the light on, and ran around the room flapping her hands excitedly. The evaluation ended shortly after that, as did any hopes I had of her doing well.

I wanted to grab both my girls and run out of the room so that I didn't have to hear what I was about to hear, but instead, I sat there in an awkward silence. As Mandy and Joni wrapped up their paperwork, I could tell that they were trying to think of a nice way of telling me that there was something wrong with my little girl. Yet, once again, their professional side came to the rescue, and they smiled warmly as one of them grabbed the tissue on the way over to sit with me.

They skillfully explained the tests just given to Danielle and told me that she seemed to have a profound learning disorder. Her language, comprehension, and social skills seemed to be the hardest hit, but all areas were technically affected. As they were talking, I was trying hard to grasp it all and still keep my composure, but my heart felt like it was breaking in two. There was a sick feeling racing throughout my body, and when I opened my mouth to speak, I could hardly say a word. As a single tear escaped down my cheek, I managed to say, "So what do we do now?"

They took it from there, and for that, I was grateful because my mind hit a blank note, and I couldn't think of much more to say. They explained to me how their program worked and that the next step would be to have Danielle evaluated by a neurologist. In the meantime, they would start her at early intervention and schedule an appointment for a behavioral specialist to come and give an assessment at the house. If ever I felt consumed by life, that certainly seemed to be the moment.

As my girls and I left the center, I was holding both their hands while walking toward the parking lot, and all at once, the reality of what was going on seemed to hit me like an unexpected line drive to the face. I felt myself starting to shake so badly I could hardly walk. By the time I reached the van, I felt as if my legs would give out beneath me. I put the girls into their car seats as quickly as I could and hopped into the front seat so that they couldn't see that I was upset.

As I stared out the car window in disbelief, the only thing I could think of was, *Why, God? Why is this happening to my little girl? Please! Help her!* And as the thoughts passed through my mind, I began to cry as if I would never stop. So, I turned up the radio so that the children wouldn't hear me, and with my face in my hands, I released as much sorrow as the moment would allow. After about ten minutes had passed, I managed to pull myself together and drive everyone home. When the children were napping, I made a few phone calls to different family members, and they did their best to comfort me.

While talking, someone suggested, "It's probably autism."

That was the first time it crossed my mind that the two could even remotely be connected. I guess I took the learning disorder to mean a little slow or something, but I never imagined autism could be part of the scenario. So, after hanging up with the family member, I called Mandy at early intervention and asked her if Danielle could possibly have autism. She said it was not their place to give a diagnosis because that was for the neurologist to determine.

So I pressed a bit more and said, "Okay. Then if it came back from the neurologist that she was autistic, would you be shocked?"

All she said was, "Anything is possible, Maggie. Let's just wait and see, okay?"

I didn't push the issue any further because I believed I had figured it out for myself. The hand flapping, the screaming for hours, and the eyes rolling up into her head—it all fit. I hated it, but it fit. *How could I not have put it together before?* I thought. To say I blamed myself would be an understatement. I began to feel an immeasurable amount of guilt and anger concerning the whole thing. I was mad at the nurse for giving Danielle the second dose of the MMR vaccine, but I was also mad at myself for somehow not anticipating her actions in the room that day.

I felt like I was losing my daughter yet had to go through the agony of watching her simply exist day by day. But most of all, I felt mad at God for allowing it to happen in the first place. However, I believe He understands us much more than we give Him credit for because, at the same time, I knew His heart was breaking as much as mine. There is a verse in the Bible that talks about God not putting any more on us than we can bear, but my feeling at the moment was that He overshot the goal this time, and I was about to pay the price for it.

I did what I had to do to get through the rest of the afternoon and was grateful when the day came to an end. I usually read to the girls before they went to bed, but because Ashley had already fallen asleep, I tucked her in and gathered Danielle in my arms to do the same. She seemed unusually restless the past week whenever I tried to hold or give her any kind of attention, but on that night seemed to have more than her usual irritability going on. I figured it was because I was upset and she could sense it, so I overlooked it and continued with what I was doing. As I laid her down and covered her up, I automatically knelt beside her little bed to pray and kiss her good night, but this time she just turned away from me as if I did not even exist.

I went to touch her again, and she quickly pulled away as if to say, *I don't want you … I don't love you.* I felt as if my heart had shattered into a million pieces inside me. She was slipping into her mind, and I could only stand there helplessly and watch. There is no greater pain to a parent than that of losing a child and not being able to help. If God would have told me that He wanted my life in exchange for hers and the moment I departed Danielle would be fine, my only reply would be, "Let's go!" Thought after thought went through my mind until I collapsed on the floor next to her, and with my face down in the carpet, I cried for what seemed like hours.

Later, as I stared at the ceiling, my mind was blank for the first time in months. I was exhausted mentally and physically, but it's at these times that God is able to meet us because He knows He has our attention. I suddenly remembered the powerful words of an inspiring teacher I knew in Bible school a few years back. She used to speak in chapel occasionally and would share about her own experiences with her son who had a rare skin disease. I would often hear her say, "Faith is like walking out on a limb, sawing the limb through and watching the tree fall!" As the words went through my mind, I felt a surge of strength go through me like a shock wave. Both the room and my heart were momentarily filled with a peace that I couldn't explain if I tried, and it was comforting in every way. I believed that God was asking me to trust Him ... no matter what I saw and no matter what I heard ... just trust. So, with that, I leaned over my little girl, gently kissed her on the forehead, and whispered, "Good night, love. Tomorrow is a new day!"

CHAPTER **5**

ANGELS?

I was up early the next morning preparing breakfast and getting everyone ready for the day, and although nothing was different to speak of, I felt an unexplainable peace deep inside me. I didn't know how we were going to get Danielle through all of this, but I knew inside that no matter what had to take place or how long it took us to get her there our little girl was going to be all right. I did not realize, however, the toll it would take on my husband and I as a family. Sometimes God's greatest gift is not to let us know what the future holds because that helps us focus on today. I had also asked God in the quietness of my heart that if my total trust was what He truly wanted, I be given one positive point on which I could focus so as not to give into the negativity that was trying to overtake my thoughts. Surprisingly, the next day seemed to shed some light on that whispered prayer while I was at early intervention.

Danielle was in the intervention playroom, and as I stood there painfully watching her through the two-way glass, a woman whom I had never seen before leaned over my shoulder and said, "Did you know that there was a woman who brought two of her children out of autism?"

I quickly spun around, as I was curious to see who was speaking to me and how she knew that my daughter had autism. "No, I didn't," I replied. "Who is it?"

She continued speaking and said it was a woman named Catherine Maurice, and the book she wrote is called *Let Me Hear Your Voice*. We talked for a moment about the book, and I glanced back through the window to give a quick check to see how Danielle was doing. When I turned around to continue the conversation, the woman was gone.

I stood there kind of quiet for a moment and then looked in the waiting room, thinking maybe she just got tired and went to sit down, but she was nowhere to be found. One of the workers passed by and asked me if she could help me with something, so I explained to them that I was looking for the parent who was just standing here talking to me (describing her in detail).

Her reply was, "Um … You're the only parent I've seen so far this morning Maggie. The other kids all came on the bus."

I felt like someone who'd just been caught talking to herself out loud, yet I knew I wasn't imagining things. So, I shook it off and went on watching my little girl through the window. She was having an extremely hard time coping with another child who was crying, which, in turn, upset the other girl, sending her into a lovely screaming fit as well. It was very hard to stand by and view from the outside, but I knew deep down that I wasn't doing her any favors if I went in to intervene. The reality was is that she had to learn to work through it, and I had to learn to let her.

At the end of the session, however, I was standing there with open arms to pick up the pieces and wipe away the tears. The staff at early intervention were always very warm and accepting of tough moments, and I always got the impression that they were behind me no matter how complicated things looked from the outside. There was no mistaking the fact that they were there for me and my child, and for that reason, I will always feel indebted to them. Before I left that day, I inquired as to whether the book by Catherine Maurice truly existed and, if so, how I could get my hands on a copy.

I was told that it did indeed exist, and any bookstore should carry it. I never did see the nice woman who told me about the book again, but my guess was that no one else did either. I've learned not to question some things but merely to thank God quietly in my heart and move on. During the following week, the assessment came in the mail from the intervention center. Danielle was now twenty-eight months old.

Danielle demonstrated personal-social skills significantly below age level. (They couldn't even put an age level on this area because it was so low.)

She demonstrated adaptive skills at the twenty-four-month level (eating, drinking, etc.) and gross motor skills at the twenty-four- to twenty-seven-month level (sitting, standing, walking, running, etc.). Danielle demonstrated fine motor skills at the fifteen-month level with a scattering of skills up to the twenty-three-month level (holding, grasping, stacking blocks, etc.).

Danielle's language comprehension abilities were judged to be at the eleven-month level (response to name, directions, eye contact, short phrases, identifying body parts, etc.), and her language expression abilities were judged to be at the fifteen-month level (verbal abilities).

Danielle demonstrated cognitive skills at the twelve- to fifteen-month level (rational abilities, including stacking rings, blocks, symbolic play, dolls, problem-solving, etc.). Her limited interest in many of the items, as well as her limited social interactions with the play facilitator, appeared to be impacting on her developmental progress.

They also recommended that Danielle receive early intervention services to facilitate her developmental progress with an emphasis on language and social skills.

It was hard to read such an assessment, but at least we were on our way to doing something. Throughout the whole ordeal so far, I had begun to share my feelings with a good friend of mine named Donna whom I had known since college. I had no idea the stability and encouragement that she would bring to my heart and life, especially in the months that would follow. As things seemed in some areas to come together and in others to fall apart, she always had a listening ear, an encouraging word, and time to pray with me before the conversation ended. I knew in my heart that God must love me an awful lot to put such a devoted friend in my life.

August 1, 1997 was a busy day in our home. Mandy came in the morning from early intervention with a gentleman named Rob, and Tammy, the parent liaison from the early intervention, came later that same afternoon. Rob ran a company called Lighthouse Services. It offered families with children with autism and other disorders the opportunity to have a personal teacher at home. The technique they use is called ABA, or applied behavioral analysis, which is an intense one-on-one home-based service better known as behavioral therapy. Rob seemed to be a very energetic and promising kind of person, and though we encountered some difficult moments later, I am truly grateful for services provided for my daughter.

The first teacher from Lighthouse Services was a wonderful young lady named Dawn who has remained a close friend to our family. Dawn is an exceptional woman with a tremendous amount of love for the children she works with, and we were blessed by her friendship as well as her expertise.

Tammy came later that day and turned out to be a very enjoyable and comforting person to talk with. She shared with me about her own daughter and how she and her husband were working together on doing the best they could at home and at school for her. She said that we as parents are the best advocates for our children because we know them better than anyone else. I was sincerely grateful for her wisdom, experience, and visits. After the initial assessment with Rob that morning, we were told that Danielle would be eligible for twenty-five hours of service a week, but because of the shortage of teachers, they would only be able to provide four hours a week to start with and increase it from there.

So everything was set, and within a couple of weeks, Dawn came out to meet Danielle and our family. She spent about an hour and a half just talking, getting to know us, and observing Danielle in her own environment. Dawn was very warm and personable, but there was no mistaking that she was there to do her job.

It was incredibly hard to have my child evaluated and stared at by a constant barrage of people, but I knew it was necessary to get her better. So, the final appointment was set for September 12, 1997, to meet with a neurologist, and because my husband had decided not to accompany me, my friend Donna agreed to go in his stead. Although my husband made himself unavailable in helping with the issues and events pertaining to our daughter Danielle, I was grateful that he kept his word about not standing in my way when getting things in place for her. He found it difficult to talk about things as they progressed, which started to bring a strange but familiar distance into our relationship. Denial, like learning disorders, is a very real thing, and when it hits a home, it's as devastating as the disorder itself. So, dissension once again invaded our home like an uninvited guest, and my heart longed for the love and comfort of my husband who seemed to be turning his back on our marriage as well as our home.

It was good, however, to see things finally start falling into place for Danielle. Still, I felt a tremendous amount of anxiety when I looked at her. When would it all end? How would she respond to a teacher at home? How many times would she have to be evaluated? Would any of this even work? It was all so scary to think about but, for now I had to keep focused. I had to trust!

CHAPTER 6

BUBBLES!

For my birthday that year I specifically bought myself the book *Let Me Hear Your Voice* by Catherine Maurice, and it was everything I had asked God for and more. I came home, and as I began to read it, I could not put it down. All these months of trying to find someone who could relate to the fears and frustrations that I was going through finally came to an exhausting halt. My heart ached within me when I read about her children and felt at times as if I were reading about my own.

Maurice said in her book that there is no quick cure or promises, and although she was right, it didn't mean I couldn't try. I had nothing to lose and the world to gain. God had touched my Danielle. I knew it, believed it, and was not about to doubt Him now. So, with the knowledge in her book along with what I was learning from Dawn and the other sources, I rolled up my sleeves and got to work.

Considering what I was reading from Maurice's book, I started keeping a personal journal that I would write in as often as I could. I didn't want good or important moments to get lost in the shuffle, and although I wasn't as consistent as I'd like to have been, I was still able to glean some pretty marked moments from those journals down the road. I would encourage anyone beginning a journey such as ours to journal as much as possible. It's hands down the best way to measure your child's progress and show a pattern of consistency or otherwise. Evaluations from neurologists, intervention centers, doctor's visits, and more are extremely important. I wholeheartedly believe in keeping any and all records from various visits, no matter how insignificant they might seem to you at the time. It's also a good practice to keep a simple notebook handy for those impromptu moments.

You would be amazed by how much your personal notes can have the ability to fill in the blanks in respect to your child's progress at times. Think about it. A doctor and/or intervention specialist sees and works with your child/children a handful of hours a week. (Sometimes much more depending on the severity of things.) Still, in all, it's a minimal amount when compared to how much that child is at home. Hence, our notes have the ability to shed some amazing light on some missing pieces to the puzzles that we are faced with every day.

Although I took a lot of notes here and there, in hindsight I always wished I would have done more. In the meantime, there was also a woman named Katie from the intervention center who came out for one hour a week to do purposeful playing with Danielle. She would bring a big bag of various toys and encourage her to play properly with them and herself.

First home visit

Danielle sat in highchair and tolerated well. Attentive to bubbles, looked toward me, and reached for the bubble wand. At one point seemed to attempt "more" to indicate desire for more bubbles. Allowed hand-over-hand assist with toys. Placed her hands over mine during pat-a-cake. Enjoyed having her toes tickled and repeatedly brought feet up to initiate more tickling. Speech: Danielle was heard to say "baby" and attempted to say "more." Frequent babbling and more reports of attempting to say "bubble." I heard her say "two" after mom said "one." Suggestions:

Continue activities which encourage Danielle to initiate interaction, communication.

During the same time frame, Dawn started to also visit our home and work with Danielle.

I remember thinking I should put a revolving door on my house because no sooner did one person leave that another one would arrive. I did, however, learn to accept it as a positive thing because it allowed me to spend more time with Ashley, who was desperately needing some one-on-one attention, (ha-ha) or was it me?

After a while when Dawn would come to the house to work with Danielle and Ashley was napping, I would sit at the top of the stairway with a box of tissues on one side and a pencil and paper on the other. This was the only way I knew of to learn as much as possible without interrupting anyone.

Whether I had tears streaming down my face or a smile from an overheard accomplishment, I kept listening, learning, and writing. It helped me to apply the ABA (applied behavioral analysis) when they left, which, in turn, gave her the consistency she needed day and night. It also helped me find out where I fit in. All those months of just standing helplessly by and watching were gone. I was her mother, and no matter what it took, with God's help we would see her through this. It was encouraging for me to finally know what my part was in all of this ... and that I could live with!

———

I remember around the end of August 1997 we had a beautiful sunny weekend, and I was desperately trying not to think about anything but the nice day that lay ahead of us. I wanted to laugh and enjoy my children for once and, in turn, have them enjoy me. Ashley was happily swinging on the swing set, and Danielle was just kind of wandering around the yard occasionally stopping to examine a bug or a blade of grass.

I had often wondered what was going through her little mind at those times but could never quite figure it out. I guess the important thing is that

I just wanted her to know that I loved her and was there for her whenever she decided to venture out from the place in her mind that she had begun to call home.

I had heard her say a couple of words here and there in the previous weeks, but they seemed more mechanical at times than anything, and there was no real feeling behind them. Although most were used in the proper context, I didn't always get the impression they meant what they should to her. As I was sitting on the slide just watching the children, I had a small bottle of bubbles that I would blow occasionally and watch as the girls would squeal with excitement trying to catch as many as possible.

On one particular occasion, however, I watched Danielle as the last bubble popped. She stood there very quiet for a moment, looking around as if to say, "Where did they all go?" Then with all the excitement in her, she ran toward me and came to a surprising halt about six inches in front of my face. She looked like she wanted to yell the words "More bubbles, Mommy!" But nothing came out. I could see the frustration in her eyes and fought hard not to let her see mine. Almost instinctively, I blew another bubble in her direction to let her know I understood, and I quietly looked the other way as if I were paying attention to something else. A moment later she reached for my arm, and as I turned my attention back to her, she looked me straight in the eyes, smiled, and tried to speak.

She stuttered a bit at first, and then with all her effort, she blurted out the most beautiful words I had ever heard my little girl say. "Bub … bub … bubbles!" I don't know who was more surprised, her for saying it or me for hearing it, though it didn't seem to matter. I jumped up and at the same time scooped her up in my arms, giving her all the hugs and kisses that the moment would allow. She said the word *bubbles*! Not because she was told to or prompted but simply because she wanted to! I laughed and cried and blew bubbles for the next hour—in the air, on the ground, and anywhere else she wanted to have them. Ashley had made her way off the swings to join us in the fun, and we had the most wonderful afternoon we'd had in months. By the time we went in the house, Danielle had proudly mastered the word *bubbles* and was all but singing it.

I called a few people who I knew would rejoice with me and proudly announced that Danielle had said *bubbles*. Although I knew the work was far from being over, it certainly seemed to brighten the moment and maybe even shine a little ray of hope our way for the future. Nonetheless, I took it as a tremendous step for Danielle and hung on to our joyous little moment when times were not so happy in the days that were to follow.

I never realized how much I took things for granted before the events with Danielle came about, but I quickly learned to appreciate and embrace even the smallest accomplishment that she would make. Children are a gift from God. Whether they have a diagnosis of some sort or are considered normal, they need to be praised, cherished, and simply loved for who they are ... our children ... our little gifts from God!

CHAPTER 7

THE DIAGNOSIS

The following Wednesday when Katie came from early intervention, I was excited to tell her about Danielle saying *bubbles*, and she was as thrilled as I had imagined she would be. We talked for a bit, and then I left them both to their work but couldn't resist standing around the corner to hear her say *bubbles* one more time.

September 3, 1997

Danielle went to the highchair ready to play. Purposeful playing with large Legos, stacking shape sorter, and busy box. (Spontaneously places the circle in proper space and activated all mechanisms but dial on busy box.) Some nice babbling and occasionally seemed to be initiating simple words. Generally avoiding eye contact until the end of the visit where she seemed to enjoy pat-a-cake. Allowed some hand-over-hand assist plus occasional brief eye contact with pat-a-cake. Positive reaction to bunny puppet. Purposefully requested bubble. Speech: imitated "up" and "peach." Responds with "two" after hearing "one."

The visit went quite nicely, and it felt good to see her have a great day. It still brought tears to my eyes to watch her, but I believed that this nightmare and all it entailed could truly be turned around if the proper things were in place and I was consistent enough when she was at home. There were times when I honestly felt like I was at war with the disorder itself. It had taken my daughter captive, and I was desperately trying to get her back. The more I saw it trying to encompass my child, the harder I worked to set her free. At nighttime, I would lay awake in bed and evaluate what we did that worked versus what did not. After sorting it all out in my head, I would simply ask God to guide me and give me the strength to get me through the next day.

The day had come for Danielle to be evaluated by a neurologist, and I was incredibly nervous, to put it mildly. My husband never said a word about the visit before he left for work that day, and it broke my heart. I could feel the horrible distance between us again but was only strong enough to fight one battle at a time.

There would come a time for he and I to work things out down the road, but for now the fight for Danielle's life consumed my thoughts, so I focused on that and put all other worries aside. As my friend Donna arrived, I expressed my concerns to her, and after lovingly listening and reassuring me that I was doing the right thing, we were on our way. The doctor's office seemed friendly, and like any other, there was paperwork to fill out and sign. Danielle was at times hard to contain, but that's when Donna, who is incredibly wonderful with children, would divert her attention. It seemed hard to do at times, but she managed to pull it off quite nicely. As we were escorted into the doctor's office, I felt a little weak but drew the needed strength from a quietly whispered prayer while we walked into the room.

Dr. Alex was tall and handsome and seemed to be quiet by nature, yet very confident of his profession. We talked for what seemed like hours, but it only wound up being an hour and a half. He asked me a hundred questions—*literally*. They ranged from asking what she ate to what she played with the most. Some seemed a bit intrusive, but all were necessary to give a proper and accurate evaluation. After asking me all the questions that were needed, he made his way carefully on the floor by Danielle, who was playing *at* a dollhouse located next to the closed door. I say playing *at* the dollhouse because she did not play with dolls and such in the usual fashion. Instead, she would line things up in front, behind, or anywhere else she could.

As we were watching the doctor trying to play with Danielle, it was all too noticeable that he was having a difficult time. The only way he could get her to interact with him was to pass the Lincoln logs she found on the shelf directly in the middle, or she would become upset and grab them back from him. Before the visit ended, he said that my Danielle had met the criteria for having a diagnosis of PDD-NOS, which is pervasive development disorder – not otherwise specified (also known as autism). I wasn't too excited to hear that my daughter had met all the requirements, but in order to get her the help she was desperately needing the diagnosis was a very crucial step.

> According to her physician, Danielle is an attractive 30-month-old girl, whose history is significant for the "Henoch Scholium Syndrome Purpuric" at the age of 14 months with a subsequent developmental delay occurring at approximately 15 to 16 months. It's unclear whether there is any causal relationship between these two events. At this juncture, Danielle is displaying delays in her language and play development. She's also displaying impairment in her social development, with limited emerging social referencing and social reciprocity, continued eye contact, and she is also displaying some repetitive type behaviors, including her mouthing of objects and finger flapping and hand flapping. It is my impression that based on these characteristics and her history and evaluation today, that

at this juncture, she meets criteria for diagnosis of pervasive
developmental disorder – not otherwise specified.

Danielle's presenting with some marked strengths as
well. Even though she's only received one month of early
intervention services, she is already showing progress in her
language development and is starting to show emerging
social skills.

I took a deep breath after reading the letter and said a huge prayer that
God would bless our endeavors to get her through all of this. The following
Sunday, after the morning service, I went up to the pastor of our church
and told him that Danielle had just recently been diagnosed with autism
and asked if he could please pray for her. I could see the pain for her in
his eyes and knew that he cared greatly. His prayer reflected his concern
not only for her but for my family, and I felt strengthened when we
parted ways. I have grown to love and appreciate Pastor Jim and his wife,
Sharon, in so many ways and will always be grateful for the friendship and
inspiration they have so unselfishly shared with us and others.

For the next couple of months, I buried myself in learning to work with
Danielle, and one of the most important things I learned to do was to direct
and redirect. When she would engage herself in a strange or stimulatory
behavior, I would direct her to do something that did not look strange and
then redirect her to do something else in the room to take her mind off
the unwanted behavior.

For example: To direct, every time she would flap her hands, I would go
behind her and grasp her at the wrists to show her how to clap and at
the same time praise her for doing a great job clapping her hands. Then
I would redirect her to color or play with a toy that was not stimulating.
By using this method, it was possible to take those behaviors that were
unacceptable (flapping hands) and turn them into something acceptable
(clapping hands).

It was a tremendous amount of work, and I was physically and mentally
drained by the end of the day, but I knew that if it worked, it would all

be worth it in the end. One day I decided to take a count as to how many times I did this procedure and lost track after one hundred times. At the end of the day, however, I would do my evaluation of what worked and what did not, give my frustrations to God, and start over the next day anew.

I would also talk at length with Dawn and Katie about how to do various things with Danielle, and they were always so willing to help and encourage me in any way they could. Having to deal with all this was an incredible challenge, and only God knew how everything would turn out in the end. Yet, I couldn't help but wonder as I tucked my little girl in at night if I would ever hear her say *mommy* or whisper in my ear, "I love you." Was I any closer to reaching into the dark room she had shut herself in? I had no answers—only questions and a strong, hopeful prayer that wherever she was she would somehow open up and let me in. Occasionally, I would have a hard time sleeping at night and often found myself sitting next to her little bed in the dark just staring at her while she slept. She looked so peaceful just lying there with only a night-light on that softly spilled across her face. Looking at her sleep, one would never guess that there was anything amiss.

One night as I was doing my usual pondering sitting next to her, she began to stir and briefly woke up. When I looked into her eyes, they were filled with a fear that only few could relate to. Almost instinctively, I reached out to her, and for the first time in months, she let me hold her without a fight. As I gently rocked her in my arms, I kissed her and softly whispered in her ears, "I'm here, sweetheart. Mommy's here, and I promise not to let you go." A moment later she drifted off to sleep, and I couldn't resist holding her just a few minutes more before putting her down. I was trying to savor the tender moment God had allowed to come my way since there seemed to be so few lately. But little did I know that there were more to come, and the next few weeks would allow me to fulfill the whispered promise just made.

CHAPTER 8

HOMECOMING!

"Danielle ... Look at me! Danielle ... Look at me!"

I could hear Dawn upstairs in Danielle's bedroom, working with her at the little table we had set up in one corner of her room. Because her eye contact was brief and sometimes less than that, working on this area was an important part of her daily program. We also found that Danielle worked better in her bedroom as opposed to any place in the house, which is where she began her time with Dawn four days a week. Dawn, who, in my opinion, was a tremendous ABA worker, started coming only four hours a week but within a very short period of time was up to six and then eight hours. Although she was due to have a child of her own, she held to her commitments and came faithfully every morning, four days a week for two hours a day. After about three or four weeks of working with Danielle, Dawn gave me her first written evaluation, which consisted of goals and objectives, as well as the current status of where she was in regard to her functioning in various areas.

The objective was what we ultimately wanted her to be able to do, and the baseline was where she began in her performance of a certain goal.

This report was for a day in September 1997:

(1) Objective: Eye Contact – In response to "Danielle, look at me" while sitting in chairs facing each other.

Baseline: 0%

(2) Objective: Object Imitation – Imitating an action with an object when presented with a teacher's model across a variety of materials.

Baseline: Unreliable data with familiar materials and action seemingly imitative but wouldn't imitate an alternative response with same materials.

(3) Objective: Gross Motor Imitation.

Baseline: 0%

(4) Objective: Vocal Imitation.

Baseline: Unreliable Data

(5) Objective: Knowing Body Parts.

Baseline: 0%

(6) Objective: To answer Yes/No – In response to, do you want this?

Baseline: 0%

(7) Objective: Grapho-Motor Imitation – Pre-writing skills.

Baseline: 0%

(8) Objective: Expressive Language – In response to, what is this?

Baseline: 0%

(9)   Objective: Requests – Initiates requests for desired objects or activities.

Baseline: 100% using vocal approximations for bubbles, cookie, Play-Doh, and sock.

(10)   Objective: One-Step Directions.

Baseline: 0%

I wasn't sure how many more evaluations I was going to be able to endure, but this one did not seem promising by any means. Dawn, however, was encouraging and explained that every child, no matter where he or she starts, usually advances quite nicely. There are no guarantees, but I still held onto the belief that Danielle was going to exceed the expectations she was presented with and more. At the same time, I needed to stay focused on the battles that we were confronted with daily.

It's good to set attainable goals, not only for your child but yourself as well. It helps to bring about the much-needed balance that is so often lacking when a tragedy such as this hit. As the weeks passed by, I was learning more and more about the incredible responsibility I was faced with and suddenly understood why babies do not come with manuals when born.

Although God doesn't tell us why these things happen, He is gracious enough to provide us with the love and courage it takes to see our children through whatever is necessary. I learned to run to Him at the end of the day and draw enough strength to get me through the next. I had always heard that people do remarkable things when faced with tragedy but never dreamed that I would someday be among those who did. At the moment, however, it was my daughter Danielle whom I considered remarkable—the long hours sitting at the table to do work and the unbelievable frustration she endured learning to deal with other children at the early intervention center. I was afraid she would fall apart under the pressure at some point but was happy to see that she was truly holding her own.

-----------◆◆◆-----------

During the week that proceeded Thanksgiving 1997, a remarkable event happened that I believe changed not only Danielle's life but mine as well. Although I don't recall the exact date the actual event took place, I assure you I will never forget the moment as long as I live.

It pretty much started out to be like any other day, which entailed going to the intervention center to play with the other children. Then, after a nap, Danielle would get up to work with Dawn for a couple of hours at the table in her room. Up to this point, I don't believe that I had seen her have such an off day. But this day was different. Everything, including her crying, was more intense. I even noticed one of her tantrums had lasted for forty-five minutes straight. As her hands flapped relentlessly and her body contorted on the floor, I could only lie next to her and softly sing as many songs as I could in hopes that God's peace would soon take over. She didn't do so well working up in the room with Dawn either.

Not wanting to do any of her work, she kept throwing things on the floor to the point where Dawn focused in on the behavior issue and left the lesson for when she was in more control of her actions. Mealtime came and went with hardly a bite of food making it to her mouth. Instead, it wound up on the floor and walls. That night I could only keep her in the tub long enough to get her wet before she was out. My heart was aching so bad for my daughter that by the end of the day I was almost physically crying in front of her. I was oblivious to the storm that was raging inside of her, and by 7:30 that night, I had to put both children to bed because I literally could not endure another moment in what I would consider beyond a frustrating day.

Most days were exhausting, but this one could have won the Nobel Prize. After tucking the girls into their beds, I came downstairs and collapsed on the sofa, so incredibly tired I could hardly keep my eyes open. Yet, as I laid there with my face planted in a cushion, silently crying out to God, I immediately felt consumed by so much pain that I began to sob openly. *I can't do this anymore! I have nothing left to give!* I felt as if we were losing the battle and my daughter was destined to be a prisoner in her own mind. In the middle of crying, I heard Ashley calling me from what I thought was my room. So, I jumped up to see what the matter was and realized it was coming from the other end of the house where Danielle's room was located.

My first impression was that she had gone into Danielle's room and woke her up, but by the time I reached the top of the stairs, I realized how incredibly mistaken I had been. Because standing on the other side of the gate was Danielle, her little arms stretched out as far as they could go as she called: "Mommy ... Mommy."

I stood there momentarily, frozen in unbelief, but quickly caught my composure, and with tears streaming down my face, I gathered her in my arms and hit my knees. She had done it! She had reached out to me. Her hug was so tight around my neck I could hardly breathe, but I didn't care. Danielle had come home, and nothing in this universe mattered more.

For a moment, while looking into my eyes, she hesitated and said, "Mommy?" As if to say, "Where have you been?"

And in response, I took her hand, placed it upon my cheek, and said, "That's right, my love. I'm mommy ... and I'm not going anywhere!"

So, after a few of the most tender moments I had ever experienced with Danielle, I laid her back down on her bed. To my surprise, she reached for me, as if to say, "Don't leave me!" So, I awkwardly snuggled next to her on the little toddler bed and gently caressed her head while she drifted off to sleep. Then, with my arms wrapped around her, my body had finally succumbed to the pressures of the day. With heavy eyes, I softly whispered, "Welcome home, my love ... Mommy missed you!

CHAPTER 9

THE RACE

When you pass through the waters, I will be with you: and when you pass through the rivers, they will not sweep over you. When you walk through the fire, the flames will not set you ablaze. For I am the Lord your God.

—Isaiah 43:2–3

There had been so many times I thought that Danielle, as well as myself, would be consumed by this monster called autism, but it appeared that God had other plans. The next couple of weeks were nothing short of amazing. Danielle seemed to respond to and absorb everything that was presented to her in every way. I was intent on keeping after her regarding her hand flapping, screaming, eyes rolling upward, etc., and when I was too tired to go back and forth from room to room, I simply gathered her up in my arms and kept on moving. The commitment was not just God's promise that He would do His part but that I would also do all that I could to ensure a bright future for my little Danielle. Her responding was nothing short of a gift from God Himself, and I was not about to throw it away because of laziness on my part.

When we were in the car, I started to make up my own learning games. For example, as we passed by a lake, I would turn my head, point toward the water, and say, "Oh, look … There's water!" Then I'd praise her for looking at the water. Now, in the beginning, she obviously would not turn her head, but I would still act as if she did and praise her anyway. As she began to respond by turning her head and then eventually pointing and speaking, I would drop my prompts and let her do it on her own. Prompts were considered things like turning my own head or pointing to something in a certain direction. Anything that cued her to do what I wanted her to do was considered a prompt. I learned that no matter where I was or what I was doing, I could use it as an opportunity to teach. So, from the time she woke up to the time she fell asleep, I made every experience a learning one.

When we walked down the steps, we would count. When she was taking a bath, I would teach her about bubbles, soap, towels, toys, and whatever else I could grab. When we were driving, we would learn about water, trees, people, and cars. When taking a walk, the lesson was about the grass, sidewalks, rocks, and sand, and when she got dressed, we would sing the hokey pokey song (You put your right arm in. You put your left arm out.) and then repeat the same process with her feet.

When we were in between all that, I would sing the alphabet, Barney songs, patty-cake, and especially "Jesus Loves Me." I didn't know exactly how far it was that she was going to go, but I figured if she knew that Jesus and mommy loved her, the rest was secondary. I didn't give in to her tantrums. I knew it would not help her in the long run, so I remained very firm when it came to them. If she could even come close to a word when asking for something, I didn't let her get away with anything short of that the next time around and always tried to encourage her to reach just a bit further than the last time.

I was told by some professional people to make sure she does things the same way all the time because autistic children have an extremely hard time with change. So, I thanked them for their advice and went with my instincts instead, which meant that I agreed in part but not in whole as to what they had told me. I believe that children need a daily routine, not a daily ritual, and my goal was to raise a daughter, not a robot. So as often as I could get to it, I would change her room around—bed, toys, everything—and to my surprise found that after a while she was enjoying it, even to the point of wanting to help the next time around.

Throughout all this I tried to make Ashley a part of everything I did. So, when I changed Danielle's room around, I would change hers around also. It worked out better that way because it made her feel a part of things, not counting the fact that she was a terrific peer imitator for her little sister. Ashley loved the part where Danielle imitated everything she did. It was like a glorified game of Simon says, and she was in charge. Ashley was always a willing participant when it came to peer imitation and other activities, and although she didn't understand the severity of the situation at the time, she was always ready and willing to help whenever the occasion arose. Exhausted did not even come close to describing what I felt like by the end of the day, but it helped me sleep better at night knowing I was doing everything possible to ensure a brighter future for my daughter.

One afternoon just before Christmastime in 1997, I happened to be in the grocery store with both Ashley and Danielle. Now, grocery stores have never been my thing, so to speak, and I have always tried to get in and get out as quickly as possible. Things, however, tend to get a bit more complicated when you add two energetic children and massive amounts of candy stacked purposefully and (not to mention) very neatly at eye level as we check out. If you manage to get past the candy shelves with most of your wits still intact, you're doing well.

On this day, I remember the cashier telling me that it might take a few extra minutes because they were short on baggers, and she would be happy to bag my groceries after she finished ringing me up. It didn't take much for me to push the grocery cart to the end of the aisle and begin bagging the groceries myself to help move things along. At the same time, there was an older man at the end of the next register doing the exact same thing with his groceries. As he was putting his items in the cart, I noticed he had a balloon sticking out of one of the bags. Danielle saw it as well and immediately looked at the man and said, "Boon ... boon," as she pointed in his direction.

Now, others might view this as nothing, but it was a huge deal to me!

For Danielle to point something out to a total stranger and then try and converse with him about it was just an incredible feat. I remember looking at the man and saying, "Oh my gosh, did you hear that? She told you, you had a balloon!" Of course, everyone was staring at me as if I were fresh off the crazy farm, but I really didn't care. I just kept praising Danielle for telling the man he had a balloon in his cart. It was such a big step for her to reach out like that, and I was incredibly proud of her for doing it. I took every accomplishment big or small to heart. She deserved all the encouragement she could get, and I wanted her to always know that I was there for her.

By December 1997, Danielle had taken quite a jump as far as her over all abilities were concerned.

> Danielle has responded well to the implementation of an ABA home program. Within the structure of one-to-one therapy, she has acquired and learned to demonstrate her skills. The introduction of a conditioned reinforcer system has been integral to Danielle's progress. The system in place is a penny board. The penny board has helped to facilitate increased in-seat behavior, attention, and responsiveness. Currently, Danielle earns ten pennies to get up from the table. On her breaks, she will participate in structured free play activities.

> The breaks from the table have provided opportunities for Danielle to utilize play skills learned at the table to a more natural setting. She has exhibited strong generalization skills during this time, manipulating family figures with a dollhouse appropriately and engaging in appropriate play with toy cars and a garage set. Danielle requires intensive instruction to increase her complexity of speech. She has substantial receptive and expressive vocabulary. Her greatest strength is her ability to utilize vocal

approximations to request a few desired items. Currently, she is learning to articulate known words more accurately.

She is also learning to request with greater complexity, so instead of using single words or vocal approximations, she is using three-word utterances such as (I want ------). Danielle has begun learning some preacademic skills identification of body parts, colors, shapes, letters, and counting. Errorless learning procedures have provided Danielle the opportunity to make gains in these areas. Although Danielle has made significant progress in her home program, it is within the structure of one-to-one teaching that she is able to learn and demonstrate her skills. Her eye contact and responsiveness can be inconsistent if reinforcement strategies are not employed or changed if necessary.

Everything seemed as though we were on the upswing, but we still had a long way to go before things would be considered stable. There was too much at stake and I wasn't going to lose my focus now. I felt like the person who had been on the sidelines watching this incredible race playing out in front of her, only to wake up one day and find that the real race was for my child's life … and I was the runner! So, I set my face toward the finish line and ran with all my heart.

CHAPTER 10

THE GIFT

Faith is not believing that God can. It's knowing that He will!

In working with Danielle day after day, Dawn and I had begun not only to build a good friendship but also to see that there was maybe a glimmer of hope for Danielle. Dawn was very good for me in those times because she helped me stay focused on the everyday problems. As hard as I tried, it was sometimes difficult to look at everything daily and keep my sanity, yet that's what was being required of me, so that's what I did.

I used to do my own little surveys from time to time just to see how Danielle was progressing, and one of these times was on December 3, 1997. At the end of the day I sat down and wrote all the words I knew she could say with total understanding: popsicle (quicycle); mama/dada; up, up; open; no-no; done; down; potty; bed; baby; gosh; paint; squish (Play-Doh); Barney (barn); Baby Bop (bee-ba); go bye-bye; I count one, two, three, four, and she would finish by saying the number five; water (wa-wa); pen; Ashley (As-shh); choo-choo train (too-too train); bear; head; nose; mouth (moufh); *moo (for cow); light (ite); tree (tee); book; foot; shoe; come on; ball; bum-bum; sock (gock); flower (wow-er); Santa (danta); and, finally, she would roar for you if you asked her, "What does a lion say?"

It always brought a smile to my face when I heard her roar because she would put so much into it. All in all, she had acquired approximately thirty-seven words in a three-month period. I was very impressed, as were those who worked with her. Things were still looking up, but the fact that she learned these skills primarily because of one-to-one teaching didn't exactly excite me as much as I would have liked. I guess in my heart I was still quietly wishing that she would be able to learn by her natural surroundings like Ashley, but I was quickly learning that it just wasn't going to happen—not yet anyway. Danielle's six-month assessment from early intervention was scheduled for December 10, and I was both nervous and excited about its arrival.

I was excited about all that she had accomplished in the past few months but nervous about how she would perform in front of more than just Dawn (the home-based worker) and myself. On the day of the assessment, however, I woke up with an incredible calm and entered the room with the much-needed confidence that I seemed to have lacked in the previous weeks. The specialists who conducted the testing that day were Joni, Jan, Katie, and Taylor. I had always been impressed when these women went to work because I could clearly see that they did not just possess the book knowledge in their field of expertise but also love for the children they came in contact with on a daily basis. I think so often people become hardened to the fact that their jobs have the potential to change a life—or in Danielle's case, create one.

As they each took turns working with my daughter, I remember thinking, *she's doing it! Oh my gosh, she's really doing good!* I had a hard time staying quiet and composed but managed to sit through the evaluation. (Although the tremendous smile on my face gave away the absolute excitement I felt for my daughter.)

After the evaluation was over, everyone took a turn writing down observations and expectations for the next few months, and when all was said and done, there was a very positive attitude in the air. Although no promises could yet be made about her future, I still took it as a giant step in the right direction and worked that much harder in the weeks and months that followed. Danielle's activity from that day are as follows:

Danielle, 33 months

December 10, 1997

Personal, Social 20–24 months. Danielle engaged in play with Katie, looked to mom for support, did well at the table and was very attentive. She was observed to be proud of her accomplishments and actually seemed to enjoy being the center of attention. She responded well to reinforcers and refocused easily when objects were removed. Pride, excitement, frustration, and a sense of humor were among the variety of emotions displayed today in the evaluation. In the area of **social interactions/ play**, it was that Danielle displays little awareness of others while in the play group room, yet when in the **gross motor room** (a favorite place), Danielle interacts with the other children. Hence, her ability to interact with other children may depend on her preference of a specific environment. Danielle cries initially when separating from her mother upon arrival to play group but is able to regain her composure after a brief period.

The intensity of Danielle's crying has decreased while in the presence of a distressed child. Recently, Danielle has begun to show compassion toward others. Most notably, in her ability to comfort her sister (hugging, lightly patting her on the back). Danielle's mother reports that she continues to test limits, and her hand flapping has decreased. Her tantrums typically occur when an object is taken away from her, which consist of falling to the ground and crying. Danielle appears to greatly enjoy tactile type stimulation such as tickling, hugging, and kissing. She was generally happy and smiling and even displayed a sense of humor occasionally. When unable to complete a task, Danielle became frustrated yet when successful at a task displayed pride in her accomplishments.

Adaptive: Danielle demonstrated skills at the 24- to 35-month level. Her mother says that she eats a variety of foods and does not have problems chewing or swallowing. She uses a fork and spoon to eat and drinks from a cup with a lid. In the area of dressing, Danielle demonstrated skills at the 24- to 31-month level. She can put on some simple clothing (hat, shoes, coat) without assistance and washes and dries her hands with assistance.

Gross Motor: Danielle displayed gross motor skills solidly at the 30-month level. She also had some emerging skills up to the 36-month level. Danielle demonstrated walking backward, climbing, and jumping off steps. She also imitated balancing on one foot for about one second. On the stairs, Danielle ascended using a step-to pattern (two feet on each step) and descended using a step-to or alternating pattern independently. She was reported to be kicking well and beginning to get the concept of throwing a ball forward with two hands. Her mother stated that she was beginning to move a ride-on toy forward.

Fine Motor: Danielle displayed her fine motor skills solidly at the 24-month age level with some skills emerging in the 24- to 36-month age range. Muscle tone in the upper extremities and shoulder girdle stability appeared to be within normal limits. She played well with a variety of precise and accurate manipulatives and a release was observed as Danielle placed a small moving windup toy on the floor without it falling.

Danielle was presented with half-inch beads for the first time and easily inserted the string into the bead but needed some help to pull the string through. She held a crayon using a cylindrical grasp in the right hand with the thumb pointed downward. Danielle imitated a horizontal line, a vertical line, and a circle.

Communication:

Language Comprehension: Danielle demonstrated language comprehension skills at the 15-month level. She responded to no-no and demonstrated understanding of some specific words and phrases. She also pointed to body parts (eyes, nose, mouth, head, feet) on herself and is beginning to respond accurately to animal sounds (e.g., What does a cow say?). Danielle was also observed to look at objects of picture mentioned (shoe) but was not observed to point to objects upon request. The preceding represented excellent progress in Danielle's language comprehension abilities since the initial assessment.

Language Expression: Danielle's language expression abilities were at the 20-month level. She was observed to communicate wants and needs by pulling her mother over to what she wanted and by using single words with a few two-word utterances. She also was observed to name objects (cup, pishie/fishie) and pictures of objects (apple, sheep, pooh) upon request. Danielle's mother reported Danielle has approximately 30-40 single words that she uses spontaneously and appropriately in everyday situations and that she is using the phrase "want _____" with the verbal prompt "I __." She was not yet observed to use pronouns such as me, mine, you. In the area of language expression there's been excellent progress.

Cognition: Danielle's cognitive skills were at the 18- to 24-month level with symbolic play skills slightly lower

(12- to 18-month level) and discrimination skills slightly higher (24- to 30-month level).

She engaged in relational and symbolic play activities as more time spent on relational play activities (stacked blocks, completed puzzle, colored with crayons, opened/closed lids to pop-up box). In symbolic play, Danielle used single schemes as she acted out familiar activities on inanimate objects (with modeling), brushed bear's teeth and then spontaneously brushed toy monkey's teeth. In the area of problem-solving, Danielle spontaneously operated a number of mechanisms on a pop-up box and attempted to activate a windup toy after observing the play facilitator. At home Danielle, can activate several items such as turning light switches and the television on and off and flushing the toilet. Danielle demonstrated memory skills by uncovering a hidden toy following a single displacement. In discrimination, Danielle clustered similar objects (spoons, clothes pins, ducks) and matched objects with related parts (cover on pot). She placed a circle, square, and triangle in a form board and nested three cups. She matched six out of six pictures and two out of six colors.

It was an awesome evaluation, especially if you consider the previous one done by the Early Intervention Center just six months before. As one evaluation after another came in, there was an underlying factor that was beginning to surface, and it was that Danielle had an incredible gift of generalizing things. Generalizing is taking an idea or object and relating it to everyday life. For example: If we were driving, she could point to and identify a car as we passed by it, and whether she saw it on a toy store shelf or in a picture book, she was still able to identify it. No matter what form it came in, she could still recognize it as being a car. This in time not only proved to be one of her greatest strengths but a tremendous gift from God Himself.

Yet in my heart of hearts, I knew that the true gift was having her for a daughter, and my prayer was that He would give me the wisdom and courage day by day to see her through this road block (if you may) that had tried to stop her from becoming the person God intended her to become from the start. And strangely enough, my heart was comforted, not because I felt *I* had a handle on things but simply because I knew He would.

CHAPTER 11

THE TRANSITION

February 13, 1998 had brought both good and bad news all in the same day. The good news was that we were going for Danielle's six-month check up at the neurologist's office, and I was elated to show him how far she had come in just a short period. Yet it was also bad because when we arrived home, we discovered that Dawn (our home-based worker) would no longer be able to work with Danielle.

She had developed some complications in the last stages of her pregnancy and was ordered to stay off her feet by the doctor. I had already met Darla, the new teacher who was to take Dawn's place, two weeks prior at my house. Darla seemed to be a very pleasant and confident person as far as her job went. I had often heard her brag about how she trained with a man named Dr. Ivan Lovas in California. He is said to be the founder of the ABA (applied behavior analysis) program, and the more I learned about this man, the more respect I had for him. His work truly proceeds him, and the children who will benefit from his programs (when applied correctly) are phenomenal.

I was told Darla would start as soon as Dawn was on maternity leave and two weeks later found myself still waiting patiently for everything to take place. After a lengthy conversation with Darla, however, I discovered that it would be an even longer waiting period than originally discussed with

Rob, the director of Lighthouse Services. It seemed that Darla was busy working with twins, and they weren't sure when she would be available to begin working with Danielle. This was not what was discussed in a previous conversation with Rob a few months back, and I was beginning to feel some anxiety about my own daughter not having a teacher. Yet, I believed that if I was patient, everything would work itself out in the end. In the meantime, I started to carry on the home-based services myself. I wasn't sure how well I would do, but I figured that it was better than doing nothing and letting her go backward.

So every morning I would get out the penny board and all the other learning materials she needed and got to work. I changed the area in which we worked from her bedroom to the dining room. I guess I looked at it as being our special place to work, which was purposefully different from Dawn's place up in her room. During the next two months, I made various phone calls to Rob and Darla, during which no final word had been given as to when exactly Darla would be starting with Danielle. Also, another pressing issue was that she would be turning three soon, which disqualified her from early intervention services and at the same time qualified her for services through the school system in our hometown.

It was a big transition not only for her but for us as a family. One day after not being able to reach a decision on the phone with Rob about a teacher, I called Mandy at the Intervention Center to discuss our little dilemma. I told her that I was thinking about looking for another ABA service provider because ours just couldn't come up with a teacher, and it had already been two months since Dawn had left.

She said she totally understood what I was feeling and would see if there was something, she could do to make this transition a better one than it was turning out to be. Shortly after our conversation, the phone rang, and much to my surprise, it was Rob himself. He said that he was very sorry for the inconvenience to our family and that he had misunderstood what I was saying.

He stated that he took my calls to mean that Danielle was not getting *all* of her hours and that he did not realize she wasn't getting *any*. He also said that Darla would be there the following week to begin working with Danielle and once again apologized for the misunderstanding that had taken place. Whether I agreed with his explanation or not was not the issue. I simply accepted his offer and left the other nonsense where it belonged—behind me. Time was of the most importance, and I didn't want to spend any unnecessary energy in the wrong direction.

There had already been kind of an introductory meeting with the school where we met and discussed possible ideas for what Danielle needed to help her continued progress. I was nervous because I had heard several heartbreaking stories about how the schools give only what they have to and no more. It boils down to one thing, I was told: money. In some cases, this really is the reasoning behind decisions that are made, and to those individuals in charge, I say shame on you, and to the parents, I say fight with everything in you to get what your child needs. I learned that we as parents truly are our children's best advocates.

This, however, was not the case at the school my daughter was to attend. I was not able to be at the second meeting because Danielle was very sick that day, but my husband (after much pleading) agreed to go with Rob (the director of Lighthouse Services) to the school meeting. They came back and informed me that they granted us everything we were asking for on Danielle's behalf. The team at the time consisted of the two preschool teachers (Mrs. Kayla and Miss Leah), a speech and language therapist (Mr. Vic), an occupational therapist (Mrs. Stevie), Katie from early intervention (one of Danielle's home-based teachers), and, most importantly, Dr. Sheri, the special education director.

From the introductions on, I could tell that my daughter was in good hands because although they were serious about their work, they were also the most caring individuals I had ever met. You could sense that their sole concern was for Danielle from the very beginning. There were questions such as: What would be the best program? What hours should she attend? What specialists were needed to help her best excel? And so on. They always held the parent's views and opinions in high regard and handled them with the utmost care and respect. The meetings that were held were called IEPs, which is short for individualized educational plan. This is where the teachers, special education director, and any other potential specialists along with the child's parents meet and come up with an educational plan for the year that best fits the child's needs per the type of disability he or she might possess.

If I wasn't happy with how a program or task was going, I could call a team meeting and discuss my concerns with them. I found that they were always open to any suggestions I had that would improve on Danielle's situation if it were necessary. So, everything was set in place, and on March 16, 1998, Danielle entered the preschool program in our hometown. Mrs. Kayla and Miss Leah were so very helpful and comforting when I brought her in on the first day. I was incredibly stressed about how everything would go as I dropped Danielle off on her first day of school (which they could clearly see), but they were extremely patient as they reassured me that she would do just fine, and she did.

While in the IEP meeting, it was agreed that we would keep a notebook log in Danielle's backpack so that we could communicate daily with each other or as needed. This way we could keep an eye on the issues at hand as they came up and address them quickly.

> Danielle had a wonderful first day! She participated in all the class activities, taking her cue from the other children and imitating the PT exercises. She transitioned quite easily, which was actually surprising, especially given her just starting. Perhaps the hardest part of the day was waiting for a turn during PT. She did fuss once, trying to get her way (cutting the line), but calmed down immediately. We were quite excited about her participation, remembering that she is always first during E.I. Center activities. We are thrilled with her, as are the children. Her eye contact was also good, especially with adults. She loved the scooter board and the jump board during PT! Danielle worked

very hard on her lion project today. We used paint brushes for gluing. A little messy if she forgets to wipe her brush, but she accepted our help. We made a penny board but didn't use it today. We may implement it during meeting time and show and tell. Hope tomorrow goes as well! Miss Leah and Mrs. Kayla

As I finished reading the note, I felt a surge of reassurance pass through me like a warm summer breeze, and I knew beyond a doubt that this was the place God had intended our little Danielle to be. So, the transition was made, and it seemed as though we had made it safely from early intervention to the public school without too much trouble. The next few months, however, would prove to be the hardest times that our little family would ever go through, and I thank God for the calm that these women brought to us during it all.

CHAPTER 12

SCREAMING SPACE?

As anxious as I was about how Danielle would handle the transition and all that it entailed, I found that it was actually me who was having the hardest time adjusting. I couldn't believe how supportive everyone at the school was, and I began to draw strength from their encouragement. When Darla started, we decided to keep Danielle's workplace where it was upstairs in her bedroom. There was no reason to change what was already in place and working well.

It took Danielle a good couple of weeks to get adjusted to her new teacher and routine, but little by little, everything seemed to fall into order at a comfortable pace. The Special Education Department was an incredible place to be, and I loved to get there a few minutes early every day when picking up Danielle, just so that I could watch her go from one activity to another enjoying herself. Miss Leah and Mrs. Kayla were always so nice to me when I came in, and whether Danielle was having a good day or a not so good day, the report was always a positive and encouraging one.

To me, it was everything a parent could ask for and more—a safe and positive environment for our child to learn and grow and peace of mind knowing that everything that could be done for her was taking place. The rest, as far as I was concerned, was up to God. I never try to do God's work; I have enough challenges just getting through a simple day in which

I am very grateful for His help! Our school system surpassed good and balanced and landed somewhere between awesome and outstanding, not because of great rules and regulations but because of the incredible love and dedication that all of the teachers possessed for the children in their care.

Darla started working in our home somewhere around the first week of April 1998. She began working on things like get ready, look at me, tracing and simple drawings, four-block imitation, two-step commands, yes questions, are you a boy or a girl?, colors (black, blue, brown), picture cues (I see a ——), emotions (happy, tired), prepositions (on, in, under), and upper-case letters.

On one particular day about two months after Darla began, I remember doing some house cleaning while they were upstairs in Danielle's room working. She was doing good and, at the same time, not so good. This simply meant that when Danielle was at the table doing her one-on-one work with Darla, she was fine. When she had earned enough pennies to fill up her penny board, her reward was free play. This meant she could play with the toy or activity of her choice for a three- to five-minute time frame, and then it was back to work at the table with Darla. It was at this point that she would fall apart to the point of throwing herself on the ground and screaming.

I didn't want to interrupt and bring more chaos to the moment, so I quietly leaned around the corner when Danielle wasn't looking and motioned to Darla that I'd be right back. I wanted to step out for a short minute and go down the road to the post office. I also needed to take a break from all the intense screaming she had been doing all afternoon. I wanted nothing more than to reach in the room and comfort my daughter, but those times rendered myself completely helpless. The truth is, it's important for parents to take some time out to get refocused.

I found that when I took the time to do this, my patience and anxiety levels were well within their healthy limits. As I pulled out of our driveway and came to the stop sign down the road a bit, I could still hear Danielle's resonating screaming in my head, and as I rounded the corner where our town baseball field was, it suddenly dawned on me that anytime we would come around this corner she would also scream the same way. The moment was a pretty profound one as I recall, so much so that I even pulled my car over to sit and really focus on things a minute or two more. I felt a bit silly for sitting there, but I just kept thinking as I stared at the empty field that there was some crazy connection between her room and the field. But what was it?

I recalled the day the year before when she first began to scream around this corner. I thought maybe she was stung by an unnoticed bee that flew in the window it was so intense. But after pulling over and checking her out, I found that she was fine. This was a mystery that taunted our lives daily.

My mind was in overdrive as I would picture Danielle in her room screaming during free play and then again as we rounded the corner where the field was. The link between the two in my mind was the screaming, but how could I fit the other puzzle pieces together so it would make sense and help her get past the fear so she could move on?

My experience as a parent thus far had taught me that our children have certain cries that differ in their intensity depending on what the issue is—for example, when they're playing, angry, frightened, or hurt. Each instance has its own sound, and as a parent, you know all too well which ones are no big deal and which ones you need to come running for. But this scream had me stumped because there seemed to be no valid or apparent reason for it.

Yet, as I sat there blankly staring at the field, I had such a profound thought I instantly knew it was nothing short of a God moment! I was in such a hurry to get home I scarcely even checked for traffic as I spun the car around and headed back down the road.

As I barreled up the driveway, the car came to a screeching halt, and I jumped out and ran inside. Upon entering the house, I went directly to the junk drawer in the kitchen and abruptly disassembled it in the process of looking for the masking tape, which was snuggly tucked in the very back.

I was so excited about my newfound revelation that I think I only hit every third step as I raced my way up to Danielle's bedroom. As I stood at the entrance to her room, I proudly smiled (while holding the tape in the air) and announced to Darla that Danielle's screaming problem was a ninety-cent issue and that I believed that I had solved the mystery.

Her first reaction was, "Huh?" Ha-ha ... and I remember thinking, *not exactly the profound response I was looking for, but hey, I'll take it.* So, I went on to explain that when Danielle had free play in the room, she would start to scream, and when we would pass the baseball field at the end of the road, she would also scream the same way. Darla quietly agreed simply by the nodding of her head. So, I continued to explain that I believed the common denominator between the two was *space*.

She stared at me for second and then yelled, "Oh my gosh! How on earth did you figure that out?"

Laughing I simply said, "When you talk to God ... ha-ha ... sometimes He answers you back!"

So, with that, I proceeded to make a small box on the floor with the masking tape. The next time Danielle earned free play, I gently put a couple of her favorite toys in the square with her and said, "Play, honey," and she did! Over the course of the next two months, I would periodically move the tape outward on all sides until there were just four small pieces on each of the surrounding walls in her bedroom that I let her tear off when she was ready.

During this time, I would also make frequent stops at the baseball field with both Ashley and Danielle. We would play on the swings, kick the soccer ball, or simply walk around while I held their hands and we all laughed. Our favorite thing to do, however, was to lie in the grass and name all the different shaped clouds that passed by. Their imaginations never ceased to amaze me with what they would come up with. By the end of the summer, Danielle's favorite place to be (as was ours) was the baseball field ... and still is today.

CHAPTER | 13

SENSORY SCARES!

On March 30, 1998, the next IEP meeting took place. Dr. Sheri led not only the meeting but the wonderful team of professionals who would be working with our Danielle throughout the coming year. Dr. Sheri was a little woman with an incredibly big heart, yet when she walked into a room, there was no mistaking who was in charge. As she began to speak, you could see this merging of absolute intelligence and pure passion at work, and it had the ability to set not only your heart but your soul at ease. I have had nothing but respect and admiration for this incredible woman and found it a privilege to have learned from her while she was the special education administrator. I know for a fact that many lives were changed for the better because of this woman's work ... including mine. During this meeting, the subject of potty training came up, and it was clearly noted that Danielle was not yet using the potty independently. The reality was that she was still in diapers and pull-ups.

In the months that preceded this meeting, Danielle had begun to be incredibly picky in her eating habits. She would literally eat only just a few things (for example, mac and cheese, hot dogs, Cheerios, and chocolate milk). There were times when I still supplemented some baby food just to make sure she was continually getting the proper nutrients. During this time, she also experienced a lot of constipation because of the pickiness of her eating habits. She was stuck on starchy foods for some reason, and it was nearly impossible to get her to eat anything else. Also, when I would take my girls to the playground down the road, I would no sooner turn my head and Danielle would start putting sand in her mouth … handfuls at a time. I would almost be gaging along with her as I scrapped as much of it out of her mouth and off her tongue as I could.

I started to bring a bottle of water with me when we visited the playground so I could wash away the grit from off her tongue and between her teeth. The saying that you have to eat a pound of dirt before you die always went through my mind, and I would think, *My gosh, what's your hurry?* It's been proven that an overwhelming number of children with autism have a hard time with textures and how things look and feel, so if it even seems weird, they will adamantly refuse to go near it, let alone touch it. I could not understand in my heart of hearts why eating sand was so much better than eating broccoli or carrots … or *anything* for that matter. But most of the time, what I thought didn't matter. What *was*, however, did matter.

At the Early Intervention Center, there were various types of rooms, including the gross motor room, the fine motor room, the craft area, and the sensory room, each of which had its own significance in the kids' daily routine. In the sensory room, there was this table that had dried macaroni and rice mixed together for the children to run their hands, toy cars and trucks, and various other toys through, just to get through the strangeness of how it feels.

This, however, didn't seem to be Danielle's problem. She would put handfuls of the dirty mix into her mouth one fistful after another, so much so that the staff would be leaning outside of the room from time to time asking me to please take the mix out of my daughter's mouth.

One woman even asked me to please feed my daughter before we came in from then on. I have found throughout the years that not everyone is as sensitive to certain moments as others, and you just need to learn not to take it personally. The reality is that they're still learning, just like you and me, and they're simply not there yet. Still, I couldn't deny their words hurt, and I would cry silently to myself and pray for God to help my daughter to be like the other children soon. However, as the years have passed by, I've learned one important lesson, which is simply this: *normal* is just a setting on a dryer. So, don't allow yourself to get upset over people who judge you (or your children) based on their view of perfection. It's okay to be choosey about who you give permission to speak into your life.

We started to take Danielle to the neurologist every six months as required. On her first visit, she was seen by a man named Dr. Alex, but after he left the practice, Danielle's case was given to a woman named Dr. Maddie. She was a little elderly woman who had the gentlest character I've ever seen in a doctor. Her soft demeanor put me so much at ease that it felt like I was at my grandma's house rather than a neurologist's office. As she began to speak, though, I was immediately taken by the pure depth of her knowledge. As I watched and listened to this powerful little woman, I found myself in awe while she spoke, so much so that I quietly made a mental note to myself to make sure my mouth wasn't just hanging open. She was not only brilliant but unbelievably encouraging too. By the time we left the office that night, I wasn't sure whether we had seen a doctor or an angel. Nevertheless, I took as much of her words of wisdom with me and applied them in as many areas as I could think of, including my heart, which she managed to encourage during our simple visit. Her report came in about two weeks later and was as encouraging as the visit.

Neurology Consultation: Dr. Maddie (7/24/98)

Danielle has been receiving home based applied behavioral analysis services, 15 hours per week since September 1997. In addition, she has been attending a center based preschool program, four times per week over the past one month and usually during the school year, and three mornings per week. Her classes consist of 10 students and is taught by approximately 2 adults. No applied behavioral analysis (ABA) is offered in the classroom. Despite this fact, Danielle has done very well in school. During the school year, there is a team-teaching approach, that has proven to be highly affective for her. During the summer, she has one teacher and 3 aides.

Danielle has received occupational therapy and speech and language services within the context of a group. The therapist tends to homework sheets, which the parent addresses themselves. Danielle's mother is continually in contact with the teachers as well as with the therapists.

Mrs. Weathersby indicates that Danielle has made excellent gains in a wide number of areas. From the perspective of language, Danielle has expanded her vocabulary and her mean length of utterance. Initially, she was speaking only in word approximations, using "coo" for "cookie" for example. Initially, attention span was poor as was eye contact. All of this has substantially improved and virtually appears to be indistinguishable from her typical peers. During the first month of school, she had marked difficulty with seat behavior, but this too has subsided. Play skills have likewise expanded and she is now using imaginary play quite well. She interacts with her sister Ashley, who is "constantly in her face." Social skills also have gained.

Areas of concern which persist, is the fact that Danielle still requires some help in initiating verbal contact with other children. Her language, however, is expanding spontaneously on a day to day basis. For fun, Danielle enjoys books, likes to play, enjoys playing with a Barbie house, and will frequently walk off with her sister's Barbie dolls. Presently, Danielle appears to be going through the "terrible two's" and her favorite word now is "no." She really likes to take a bath, enjoys swinging, and will frequently ask her mother to "push me." She enjoys singing and can sing "Jingle Bells." She also enjoys "Mickey Mouse." Behaviorally in the past, Danielle has had difficulty with screaming and hitting behavior. Now she is showing increased empathy and is aware of the emotions of others, particularly if appear to be sad. Motorically, she has also made gains. In the past, she was a frequent "W sitting," but this has subsided as well. Danielle's educational plan indicates that she'll be attending the local Center School in her town. The educational plan calls for a 502.8 prototype, in which she's scheduled to receive three classroom sessions per week, speech and language services twice weekly in a direct level and one session in a small group, in the classroom.

Danielle is a very pretty little girl, who comes readily to the examining room. Her height is 37-1/2 inches, her weight is 28 pounds. Her general physical examination is unremarkable and there's no obvious dysmorphic features. Eye contact seems to be good and language self-initiated.

Very little echolalia was observed in contrast to her previous assessment performed by Dr. Alex in February of this year. Spontaneous language now appears to be much more appropriate and focused. Hand dominance has not been well established and she generally appears to be ambidextrous.

Motorically, she shows generally good muscle bulk and strength, but tone appears to be mildly reduced throughout, with some hyperextensibility, particularly at the wrists and ankles. Deep tendon reflexes are 2+ and equal and plantar responses are flexor. Her gait is normally based but continues to seem some awkward with some hyperextension of the knees. Occasional toe walking persists but is not consistent.

In summation, Danielle's now a 3-year 4-month-old child with a diagnosis of (PDD/NOS) Pervasive Developmental

Disorder – Not otherwise Specified. She's continued to make excellent gains, both socially and in language, as well as in pretend play skills. Motorically, she's gaining as well. This fall, it's expected that she will enter a small integrated preschool program but will continue to receive speech and language support within the context of this program. Although Danielle's made excellent gains, it should be noted that children at this level have skills which are still distinctly fragile. Failure to continue to provide the support systems which have allowed them to make these gains, runs a substantial risk of significant regression during this period. Therefore, every effort should be made to continue the level of services, previously provided to Danielle for at least one additional year.

Recommendations:

1. We totally support Danielle's placement in an integrated preschool program as currently designed by her educational plan.

2. It is strongly recommended that Danielle continue to receive substantial speech and language services. Danielle needs to be monitored carefully.

3. Danielle needs to be evaluated by a pediatric occupational therapist certified in sensory motor integration. As far as her issues with low muscle tone, motor planning, body and space awareness, and perceptual skills all need to be assessed, as well as issues pertaining to sensory modulation

4. Danielle's progress should continue to be monitored and she should be seen for a repeat evaluation in approximately six months' time. Constant monitoring,

titrating, and readjustment of her programs are necessary to ensure ongoing gains and progress.

So, within a very short amount of time, the evaluations started to pour in one by one from every expert our school system had to offer. I loved this school because they all took such pride in caring not only for Danielle but for each child in their room. Dr. Sheri would check in periodically with me to see how things were going with Danielle and never cut me short on the phone as I would go through all my excitement as well as my concerns about her progress. Instead, she would just take the time to really listen, and at the end of our conversation, she would encourage me to continue on and not lose my focus. What a wonderful example she was to those around her.

I learned during the first years of Danielle's diagnoses that any information I could obtain about autism wasn't just going to fall out of the sky. I had to do lots and lots of research, make plenty of phone calls, and much more. It was all worth it in the long run, no question about it. It kept me on my toes, to say the least. Anything you can learn about your child's disorder is an incredible asset not only to the child but to the whole family as well. So, don't be afraid to dive in. Having knowledge of your child's disability actually has the ability to put you back in the driver's seat, which is exactly where you belong—not just for your child's sake but yours as well.

CHAPTER 14

POST-TRAUMATIC POTTY TRAINING!

The mere mention of the words *potty training* in general has the ability to send most parents into a frenzy, while the other half somehow courageously stand their ground and say, "Let's do this thing!" I wish I could proudly say that I was among the courageous, but I actually fell between the procrastinators and those who like to declare, "Today's just not a good day." On my list of favorite things to do as a mom, this would probably fall into the *not* category. But like any loving mother, I gave myself a pep talk ... and fixed myself a bowl of ice cream.

I had thrown myself into helping my daughter on the academic level so much that I was almost oblivious to the fact that Danielle wasn't potty trained yet. Sometimes, I was so exhausted it felt like my whole body was miles behind my to-do list. Nevertheless, it needed to be addressed, so I dove in. I spoke with the team at her school and with Darla, who was still providing home-based care, so that everyone was on the same page. In June 1997, we starting to potty train Danielle. It was no secret that Danielle was a picky eater; many children are naturally. But the downside to only eating starches is that it has the distinct ability to bind you up, which is very often what happened.

I had to give her a half of a suppository every now and then (as prescribed by our pediatrician) because she would get so backed up. It really tore me up inside to see her in pain like that. I used to think to myself, *no child should have to deal with this kind of stuff at such a young age!* Yet, here we were.

So the day came when the potty chair was brought out, and I was as encouraging as I could be. I even bought her favorite candy for incentives. As the morning got underway and everything was introduced to her, she seemed to be doing very well. I was starting to really feel good about things. I even put the potty chair in her room with her and Darla to keep her on task with her work. As noontime was approaching, I was downstairs in the kitchen making her lunch, and I began to hear her cry. At first, it just sounded like her normal it-hurts-to-go cry, and I recall walking around the kitchen praying for God to help her to go soon as I was preparing her food.

But after about five minutes, she began to scream so intensely that I decided to head up the stairs and further investigate the issue. Once in the room, I knelt beside her as she sat on the potty chair. I began to speak softly to her as I gently rubbed her back. As I leaned over to look in the potty and see if she had gone yet, I saw the most disturbing sight ever. At first glance, it looked like she was in the process of having a bowel movement, but when I took a closer look, it was actually this long, bloody-looking tissue coming from her bottom. I remember wanting to reassure her that everything was okay, and that mommy was going to make it all better, but I was literally in shock myself.

Although incredibly stunned, I forced myself to problem-solve instead of panic, which, to be honest, seemed like the better idea but not practical on any level. I told Darla to go get me a towel out of the closet so I could wrap it around my daughter's bottom. It just made more sense than trying to put a pull up on her while we drove to the hospital. On the way there, Danielle collapsed into an exhausted sleep from crying so hard.

My heart was in tears as well, but I had to keep my emotions contained on some level at least so I could legibly talk to the doctor when we arrived at the hospital. Shortly after arriving at the ER, we were taken into one of the little rooms where I just held Danielle in my arms until they came in to check her. As the doctor stepped in the room and began to check her out, Danielle woke and started screaming so hysterically I could hardly hear what was being said. I did my best to caress and console her throughout the examination, but my efforts seemed pointless for the most. Her screaming was so intense she was literally sweating and hyperventilating at the same time because of the pain. I remember being so terrified by the way it looked I could hardly even think of what questions to ask the doctor next that would remotely sound intelligible. As he finished up his examination, I scooped Danielle up in my arms to comfort her, and she quickly collapsed on my lap and fell asleep again.

The doctor told me that Danielle was tremendously backed up and needed to see a GI specialist the very next day, which he was writing a prescription for as we spoke. He also told me that Danielle had what they call a rectal prolapse. I looked up its meaning when I got home that night, and the dictionary defines it like this: "Rectal prolapse is caused by weakening of the ligaments and muscles that hold the rectum in place." I recall thinking that I would have rather not known its meaning once I read it.

Nevertheless, we somehow made it through the night, and I found myself sitting at the specialist's office with Danielle by nine thirty the very next morning. Dr. Ellen was anything but warm. She spoke in big, overbearing terminology that only a premed student could understand and seemed quite put out that I had the audacity to ask her to break her explanations down into simpler terms. She said that Danielle had experienced a prolapse due to her bowels being so impacted. She ordered a molasses enema (to be given immediately in the office) and told me that she would be in to check her again after it was given. If Danielle wasn't traumatized by the so-called prolapse the day before, the enema certainly had the potential to bring it home. I remember thinking, *my gosh, how can this little, bitty child possibly survive all this terrible pain?* I mean, it wasn't even happening to me, and I was in agony just watching her!

The enema helped, but it was horrible to see my little girl suffer like that. As Dr. Ellen came back in the room, she said that she was putting Danielle on something called Lactulose (latch-a-lose) and some other disgusting medicine to keep her cleaned out and flowing. She said I needed to give the medicine to her daily and that she wanted to see Danielle back in her office in a week. The way she spoke down to me was incredibly intimidating, and I left her office that day feeling like the worst mother in the world. I remember thinking, *Wow, for someone who's in the healing business, she sure did a lot of damage emotionally!* However, on the flip side of this statement, I feel the need to acknowledge that I have met some amazing doctors, pediatricians, and specialists along the way. And because the good doctors far outweigh the bad, I choose to take their words of wisdom with me as opposed to the heartless words of the minority.

Every morning I made chocolate milk in a sippie cup for Danielle, so I started putting the Lactulose in it and just kind of mixed it all up and handed it to her to drink. It was a disgusting mix of what looked like oil and lighter fluid. It smelled like it too. It didn't take Danielle long to start refusing it. Within a couple of short weeks, Danielle was almost eating nothing at all. The medicine that the doctor had prescribed made her stomach so upset that she had virtually no appetite.

I called the doctor's office several times to speak to Dr. Ellen about it but was only able to actually speak with her once. As I was trying to explain to her what was going on with Danielle, she cut me off by saying, "I'm sorry, Mrs. Weathersby, but it's not uncommon for your daughter to go through a loss of appetite; however, I expect that the protocol that's been put in place should remain in place." And with that, she said she had other phone calls to make and quickly hung up.

I remember thinking, *there's got to be a better way than this, and I'm going to find it!* I couldn't bear to see her suffer one more day on that disgusting medicine, especially from a woman who cared nothing about how her so-called protocol was affecting my child.

So, I desperately prayed and problem-solved for a few days but still came up with nothing. Then the following week during the middle of the night I woke up and remembered a roommate I once had in college. Her name was Carol (most called her Dee). Her mom's name was Vera, and she sold natural vitamins. She was an incredible woman of God. I loved going to my friend Dee's house on periodic school breaks and visiting with her family. Anyway, I could hardly wait for the sun to rise the next day. I just knew in my heart that God brought Dee's mom to my mind to help me get through this issue with Danielle.

Once on the phone with Vera, I simply explained what had been happening with my daughter and where I needed her to be. She was amazing! She told me that there was something called Herb-lax. It was a natural stimulant as opposed to the oil-based Lactulose that had been prescribed by Dr. Ellen. So, after we talked a bit more, she said she was sending me a bottle of it out the next day. I spoke to my pediatrician about the changes I wanted to make regarding the medicine she was taking, and he agreed that it might be worth a try since the Lactulose was obviously doing more harm than good. As soon as the Herb-lax arrived in the mail, I started her on it immediately. My pediatrician helped me figure out the dosage, and I went from there. Herb-lax was this dark brown tablet that would become a powder like substance if you mashed it down with a spoon or knife.

So I started her out with a half a tablet two times a day. I would put the powdery mix in her favorite yogurt and manually feed it to her during breakfast. It took a couple of days to start working, and the results were better than I had anticipated. By this time, it had been close to two and a half or three months since the first prolapse occurred. Danielle had several more prolapses but, after about the third trip to the emergency room, I had done more research and had also paid close attention to how the doctor pushed it back in when we went. I actually started pushing it back in myself at home. I would always wear the proper surgical gloves (I picked them up at our local pharmacy) so that I wasn't putting her in danger with any bacterial infection or worse. As Danielle started to have easier bowel movements, the prolapses started to slow down. She was terrified of sitting on the potty because of all the trauma that surrounded it, and who could blame her!

Still, my goal was to take the fear out of going to the bathroom ... and I didn't have to be Einstein to figure out it was not going to be an easy task. I used to think the odds of success would be higher if she were skydiving without a parachute. But that's what needed to happen for her to be potty trained ... so that's what I did. It was about a month after we started her on the Herb-lax that she actually had her first successful experience on the potty chair, and I assure you, we were *all* singing the pee-pee-on-the-potty song!

Ashley continued to be the most amazing role model for her sister. Her love and devotion as a big sister remained epic as they grew up.

I remember thinking, *God, you were so gracious to bless me with such an incredible firstborn child.*

Within a month of Danielle starting to go on the potty on a somewhat consistent level, my pediatrician referred us to another specialist (to take the place of Dr. Ellen). His name was Dr. Todd. Still reeling from the horrible-mom complex Dr. Ellen had so wonderfully left me with, I was imagining this doctor might mirror her actions, but I was about to learn a great lesson in assuming.

In fact, ten minutes of talking with Dr. Todd in his office humbled me almost to the point of tears. Although I was apprehensive at about divulging the protocol, I had Danielle on, his calm and welcoming demeanor instantly put me at ease.

He asked me about her daily routines, what she ate, what she watched on television, the toys she played with, her friends, her sleeping habits, and so much more. As I explained what I was doing and how much Herb-lax I was putting in her milk each day, he simply said, "You're doing a great job, Mom. Just do more."

He suggested that instead of giving her half a tablet two times a day, I should give her a whole tablet two times a day. And as she started going more frequently and more easily, she would begin to lose some of the fear associated with going to the bathroom in general, which was the intended goal from the start. As exhausted as I was by the end of our visit, I was also excited and, more importantly, encouraged. I was ecstatic because he wasn't just a good doctor; he was an easy, down-to-earth person to talk to. I wasn't judged or ridiculed for using my better judgement. Instead, after looking over her charts for a moment, he said, "Good job, Mom!"

I remember thinking … *Wait! Did he just say good job to me?* I had continually heard things like: "You're not doing it right." "You're not following protocol." Or, my favorite, "Moms are not professionals; doctors are!" Dr. Todd taught me that following my mommy instincts was one of the best things I could do for my children. Why? Because typically we know our children better than anyone else. (Of course, it's always a good thing to bring these instinct moments to your doctor's attention to make sure you're on the right road.)

I learned that as parents, we are our children's best advocates. I will always be grateful for the knowledge and encouragement he gave to me during this tough time in our journey. It took about six months altogether to get Danielle potty trained, but by the grace of God she did it! It will forever be etched in my memory the day I walked past the bathroom (not realizing anyone was in there) as I overheard a couple of little voices just chattering away in a delightful but purposeful conversation. One was humming a tune, while the other was talking in a very teacherlike manner. Leaning around the corner to further investigate, I saw Ashley on the big potty accompanied by Danielle, who was contently sitting on the child-sized potty right next to her. Ashley was softly encouraging her not to be "ascared, cuz it won't hurt you." The moment only lasted about forty-five minutes, but I enjoyed just listening to them both laughing, talking, and eating a new bag of M&Ms. (They thought I wouldn't miss the M&Ms.) I loved it!

I've had many wow moments as my children were growing up, but this one has always stood out in my heart as being one of the best. God knew Ashley was the only one who could adequately get the job done—and to perfection, I might add. I never got caught up in the idea that *I* had to be the one to do everything. Winning tough battles like this really helped to put things in perspective. It's the same feeling you get when you stand on a beach and look out at the ocean to see its breathtaking beauty and you know beyond a doubt, that without God, it just wouldn't be what it is. Moments like this were like a sweet kiss from God to let me know I was on the right track and that He would always have my back.

CHAPTER 15

MY STRENGTH

There's a song that I would listen to almost obsessively during the toughest years of Danielle's autism. It's sung by the very talented Leslie Philips, and the song is "Strength of My Life." I loved listening to her music in particular because (to me) the songs were powerful and really ministered to my hurting heart. The last couple of verses in this song went like this:

> Each day has its problems, it's troubles and its fears,
> And it seems I'm always anything but strong, but when
> I learn to know my weakness, I understand your strength
> And even when the hard times, last so long, I won't try
> By myself, I'll just ask for your help, each day

I loved the whole song in its entirety, but for some reason, when the last verse was being sung, it would literally bring me to tears ... every time! I'm quite sure it was because of how my heart ached daily for Danielle to be free from this monster called autism. The truth was, as incredible as our team and support systems were with her (and trust me, they were), my parental heart still quietly ached for her to be outside playing in the yard with her sister and the neighborhood kids, not sitting at the Little Tikes table in her room upstairs, rehearsing "Danielle, look at me," for hours at a time while screaming to the point of exhaustion. Sometimes the depths of her frustration embraced the depths of mine ... and we would just cry together in agreement.

Even though I would gently caress her face and tell her I understood how hard this must be, the truth was that I really didn't know what she was going through. How could I? But what I did understand was that it was frustration magnified by a million, and that was enough to ignite my heart. I found that when I released my pain and fears to God, I was better equipped to help her with hers, which wound up being another positive in both our healings during this crazy, unpredictable journey.

I learned quickly that guarantees only came with washing machines, and if I wanted my child to have any kind of future, it wasn't going to happen by osmosis, and even then, there were no promises. Having the right people, programs, specialists, incentives, and more is of the utmost importance when battling autism—or any kind of disorder, for that matter. But, for me, the most crucial ingredient that preceded even these was prayer. I used to hear people throughout my life say over and over (to the point of irritation, if I were honest) that prayer changes things. None of these words hit home, however, until I had children of my own.

I learned that prayer was the single-most important thing I would do, *every day*! And not as the last resort either, no matter if I was stressed, overwhelmed, or whatever the moment brought, I'd stop right there and pray, asking God for His wisdom and guidance. My job was simply to trust and be patient enough to wait for the answer. It might have come in unexpected ways, but it was always there waiting right on time.

Meanwhile, the (home-based) behavioral evaluation from Lighthouse Services came on July 22, 1998.

Even though evaluations can be redundant and somewhat repetitious, they're actually quite key to putting certain behavior patterns, both negative and positive, into their proper perspective and makes it possible to keep track of wanted and unwanted behaviors.

Behavioral Education Assessment and Consultation Inc.
Lighthouse Services
(Facilitator: Darla)
Progress Report for Danielle – July 22, 1998
Current Programs:

1. Attending Skills:

Danielle will make eye contact when given the instruction, "Look at me." 90% of the time. Eye contact is also consistent when addressing Danielle by name. Danielle is continuously working on staying with an activity until the command, "All done." is given.

2. Imitation Skills:

Block Patterns: Danielle's currently working on block structures with 4 blocks. She is successful 80% of the time.

Simple Line Drawing/Tracing: Danielle is presently working on diagonal lines, smile faces, and tracing a square. She is successful 90% of the time when she is given light wrist support.

3. Receptive Language:

Two-Step Instructions: At this time Danielle is successful 80% of the time. The first action is completed in her chair, and the second action is completed out of her chair.

What Is Missing? Danielle is successful 80% of the time with two objects.

Pretending: Danielle is presently working on community service people. Example: a fireman, doctor, mailman, teacher and a hairdresser.

4. Expressive Language:

Personal Questions: Currently Danielle has mastered her name, age, her sister's name, hair color, town, mother's name, how are you? favorite drink, father's name, school's name, and her last name. She is now working on her teachers' names.

Simple Sentences: At this time Danielle is working on "I see a ____ and a ____." She is given picture cues as a prompt and is successful 90% of the time.

Prepositions: Danielle has mastered on, in, under, next to, and on top. This week Danielle will be introduced to "in front of."

Attributes: Danielle has mastered big/little, up/down, fast/slow, open/closed, and empty/full. She is working on near/far and is successful 60% of the time.

Why/If Questions: Danielle is successful 80% of the time with ten combinations, like, "Why do you smile?" "I am happy." "What do you do if your happy?" "I smile."

Function of Body Parts: Danielle is currently working on eyes, nose, and ears. She is successful 70% of the time.

5. Pre-Academic Skills:

Numbers: Danielle can identify the numbers 1, 4, 5, 6, and 8 and is working on counting objects up to five and pointing to each object as she counts. She is able to count to thirteen independently.

Letters: Danielle has mastered the upper-case letters. Presently, she is working on lower-case letters, which she can identify about 80% of the time.

Same/Different: Danielle has mastered items that are the same. She is working on different and is successful 70% of the time.

More/Less: Danielle is currently working on "More" and is successful 50% of the time.

6. Mastered Programs:

A. Yes/No Questions
B. Colors
C. Emotions (Happy, Sad, Angry, Silly, Surprised, Tired, and Scared)
D. Action Words
E. Shapes
F. Body Parts

I was always excited when I received positive evaluations like this one. In fact, I recall it being a Friday night. I was in the kitchen where I had just finished cooking dinner. I offered Darla a quick bite to eat, but she politely declined, stating she had previous plans, and left. Later, as we were eating, I started reading over the list of mastered accomplishments and was thrilled to see how much the list had grown. As dinner went on, I leaned over to Danielle and said, "Wow, kiddo! You're really doing a great job with Miss Darla! I quickly glanced at one of the mastered skills on the list and asked her, "Can you show Mommy *surprised?*"

I was excited to see her best surprised look, but instead, she just kind of looked at me like I said nothing at all. I thought, *Hmm ... Maybe she's just tired from working all afternoon.* So, I put everything aside and went on with our night. The next afternoon, however, before we left to go to the playground at the end of the road, I asked her to show me *surprised*, and again, she just stared at me. Almost immediately, I said, "Okay, can you show me *tired?*" And I was given the same blank look.

I picked up the paper that I had left on the kitchen counter and rechecked the mastered list (thinking maybe I was just looking at the wrong page), and sure enough, I had the right one. I randomly questioned her about some other things on the list, and her responses were definitely not in line with the mastered level as indicated on the recent evaluation.

So, when Monday morning rolled around, Darla arrived. After greeting her, I expressed how impressed I was with Danielle's evaluation. She just said, "Yes, she really is doing great, isn't she?" And she turned to head upstairs where she and Danielle worked.

As she was in midmotion to turn away, I said, "Hey, if you don't mind, before you head upstairs, could you just go over a couple of the mastered skills on this paper for me? I'd love to see her do one or two if it's not too much trouble."

Her reply was, "I'd like to, but I really I need to get upstairs and get started because I have to leave a few minutes early today."

I was a bit more insistent as I said, "I promise not to take up too much of your time. I'd really appreciate if you could have Danielle do a couple of the scenarios from the mastered list down here, and with that, I quietly pointed to "show me surprised."

Darla was a bit reluctant at first, but after seeing the determination in my eyes, asked Danielle to show her surprised. Sure enough, Danielle just stood there and stared at her as well.

I then pointed to "show me tired," and when Darla asked her to show her tired, again she just stared at her like she had with me the Friday before. I had her go through a few more items on the supposed mastered list. Some of them Danielle could do, but most she couldn't.

Darla immediately insisted it was because she was used to doing them in her room, but by then, my tone had shortened, and my words were undeniably filled with irritation. I said, "Correct me if I'm wrong, but I've always taken *mastered* as meaning it doesn't matter where you are or what you're doing, you should still be able to perform the task!" I explained that I didn't appreciate the exaggerated paperwork and that I'd rather see realistic results at a lower level than the fabricated ones I was looking at on this paper. I was upset but composed, and after a moment of awkward silence, I suggested we continue Danielle's lesson tomorrow and that she was free to go and handle whatever errands she needed to do that day.

I was staring at the evaluation I still held in my hands as I heard Darla's car pulling out of the driveway. I was so upset over everything that had just taken place I almost didn't even know how to react. I felt a plethora of emotions that seemed to bottleneck somewhere between my mind and heart. Yet, this wasn't solely about my anger. To me, it was more about the deception and betrayal that our family was left with in the wake of her fabrication. Darla was recording very important data in which she was supposed to be incisive and truthful. When working in other people's homes, your integrity should be at its best. Still, the damage was already done, and I had to make a choice. Do I stay angry to the point of it hindering my direction? Or do I leave it behind us and keep moving in a forward direction?

So, after a good cry, I pulled myself together and called Rob (the director at Lighthouse Services) and explained all that had transpired. I was determined not to let my anger get the better of me, so I simply asked that we be assigned another home-based worker and left it at that. He was very understanding and switched Darla with a wonderful girl named Janis. We liked her right from the start. At our initial meeting in our home two days later, Janis and I sat and talked for a good hour and a half.

I asked her if she would be willing to go over the previous home-based worker's data, checking for any inconsistencies and bringing Danielle up to speed, no matter how far back we had to go. I can't say that I was prepared to see all the data that had been falsely recorded, but at least I knew where she stood and where we needed to go.

I'm quite sure it took me longer to forgive Darla than it did for Danielle to catch up. But the truth was, this wasn't about me; it was about my daughter, and I had to push hard to keep things in their proper perspective. Although it was a bit of a setback for Danielle, she really adjusted well to

Janis, and once again, we were moving in a forward direction. It was a real wake-up call on my part to make sure I was paying attention to how efficiently things were being done, which was epic to her progress. I used to think to myself, *So much drama! So little time!*

The real victory for me, however, was not only in allowing myself to forgive Darla but also to make a deliberate choice to stay the course.

CHAPTER 16

RESTORATION

We are hard pressed on every side, but not crushed; perplexed, but not in despair; persecuted, but not abandoned; struck down, but not destroyed!

—2 Corinthians 4:8

There were so many times during the past couple of years when I seemed to just drift from one issue-filled moment to the next. I was never a fan of drama, but there were moments when I literally felt like a live version of the latest sitcom. My energy was totally and completely spent, and I was desperate for God's help in every direction. My prayers at night were short but powerful. They started with, "Help me. I have nothing left to give!" and hopelessly ended with, "Please heal my child!" The cry of a mother's heart is nothing to scoff at, though, for we are both determined and sincere about reaching the heart of God for our children.

Things in our home life seemed to erupt as well. After a brief but intense confrontation with my husband, we separated for the second time in our marriage. Being two and a half months pregnant did not sway me from standing up against the control issues my husband was zealously displaying. Whether it was his frustration over not knowing how to help or anxiety over not being able to cope with it all, I really wasn't sure, but clearly, he was not coping. Control is a funny thing. Some people handle it so elegantly; their lives almost seem to reflect the grace and expertise of a gifted conductor portraying this beautiful dance. While others seem to simply struggle just getting out of bed without beating their pillow to death in the process. Kind of like a Mozart versus AC/DC mindset.

My personal opinion is that it's okay to be one or the other, or even a little bit of both. It's our differences that build character and make us the unique individuals we are. How we choose to deliver those differences, however, is where the struggle lies. Nonetheless, I just knew that I had come to the end of my rope trying to fight the battle of autism while confronting these issues in the same moment.

In total honesty, I would have given my right arm to have my husband come home at night and just give me a hug, a supportive look, or even a kind and listening ear. That would have been enough to keep me going for days, but unfortunately, that was not the case. Although I was aware that millions of families struggled with similar circumstances such as ours, it didn't make it any easier to live with. I had hoped that we would both somehow figure this thing out as we went along, but it was more than obvious that we were not there yet. So I had to focus on what was and not what I desired it to be. Being a single parent for most of my pregnancy while raising two other little ones was no easy feat and certainly not what I would have chosen for our little family. It was, however, my reality at the time.

I started to do some piece work from a local factory to earn gas money, which helped around the edges but by no means paid the bills. I was very grateful for all the love and support I received from my family and friends during this time because it helped me continue to focus on what mattered, which was my girls and the little one on the way.

One afternoon about a month and a half before my due date, the pastor of my church stopped over at the house to speak with me. He shared that he had been counseling my husband for the past month or so and felt that he seemed very sincere in his efforts of working toward putting our marriage back together. Pastor Jim and his wife, Sharon, were good people, and I trusted their hearts when they prayed that God would bring healing and restoration between my husband and me. Growing up in a home that offered divorce as its only choice was unquestionably not what I desired for my children. So, I agreed to join the counseling efforts and try to make our marriage work. Our separation lasted about five months, and we were reunited exactly one month before I gave birth.

Approximately four days before Danielle was to turn four years old, I gave birth to my third little angel, Shannon Rose, and she was every bit as beautiful as her sisters, Ashley and Danielle! It was love at first sight, and her older sisters adored her.

When Shannon was about a week old, I recall one afternoon when I was desperately wanting to take a much-needed shower, so I got creative and had the two older girls head up to their room and put the baby gate across the doorway. They were surrounded by all their toys, and more importantly, they were safe. I put Shannon in her infant car seat and took her into the bathroom with me. My shower lasted a total of ten minutes, and I hurried up to the girls' room afterwards to make sure all was well.

On my way up to their room however, I noticed some Barbie-doll-looking hair pieces on several steps. By the time I reached their room, I had a good-sized handful of this doll's hair. All I could think was that there was a seriously bald Barbie doll somewhere in the house. I couldn't figure out for the life of me where it had all come from, but the minute I stepped into their room, my confusion ended. Because right in the middle of the room was Danielle (slowly spinning in a circle), and all the while, she was cutting her hair off on every side with a pair of Ashley's scissors from her school bag! Ashley must have seen my look of utter despair as she ran toward me to explain that they were playing barber shop, and Danielle was the barber. As I turned my attention back to Danielle, she looked up at me, dropped the scissors, fell to her knees, and with her hands covering her face exclaimed, "Mommy, I good!"

I was mortified that her beautiful curls were gone but laughed nonstop at the whole scenario. I knew beyond a doubt that this would be among the best stories repeatedly told at our family gatherings in years to come.

June 1, 1999 was another continuation of our drama-filled lives. The temperature was a whopping 100 degrees, and it was too hot to take a little newborn outside. Yet, the girls were wanting to go out and play in the water. So, after much pleading on their part, I worked out a compromise and set up the sprinkler just outside our television room window. The proximity was incredibly close, and all I had to do was open the window to talk directly to them, which I avidly did. That way, I could watch them play and keep the little one safe from the heat at the same time.

Everything was going great, and I was quite pleased with myself until Ashley decided to pick Danielle up and run around in the sprinkler while holding her. Danielle was laughing hysterically, but as I watched Ashley slip and slide a few times here and there, I leaned out the window and asked her to please put her sister down so she didn't fall and hurt herself. One could never accuse Ashley of not being obedient because the minute I asked her to put Danielle down, she did just that, meaning she literally dropped her where she stood.

The scream that came from Danielle was not the kind of scream that you wanted to hear at all! As I bolted out the door to pick her up off the ground, I remember making a conscious mental note to interject the word *gently* the next time I was requesting Ashley to do something. As it turned out, Danielle had hit her elbow on just the right spot when she fell to the ground, which resulted in a hairline fracture. Ashley felt so bad she cried as much as her sister did all the way to the hospital. And Shannon (who was the best sleeper in the world) slept through it all! It was a long night at the emergency room, but we somehow made it through, and Danielle had a very pink (her favorite color) cast to show off for all her troubles. And, of course, Ashley was the first to sign it! It was beautiful to watch them become best friends, and this was certainly one for the books.

Occasionally, I would come into the television room and think how wonderful it was that the girls were playing so nicely with each other and pushing their dolls in the strollers only to realize that they had finagled little Shannon into one of them and were, in fact, fighting over who was going to push her into the makeshift grocery store they had set up in the playroom. As always, Ashley won. But only until I came into the room and rescued Shannon from the perils of her older sisters.

Danielle's vocabulary had taken quite a jump, and she was now putting short sentences together with greater comprehension. Her progression went like this:

Once her utterances (verbal approximations) were turned into simple words, we proceeded to turn her simple words into simple sentences. For instance, when she wanted something like a cookie, I would preface the request with "I want" or "I need," and she would finish the rest of the statement.

A simple scenario:

I would say, "I want," and she would finish the sentence by saying, "cookie." I would praise her wonderfully and say, "Great job for telling Mommy what you wanted," and then give her the requested item (and, of course, a big, healthy hug). It's important that you not only praise the child for accomplishing the desired task but also that you verbalize what the task was that the child just accomplished. Your praise should be immediate and enthusiastic.

As Danielle got the hang of that scenario, I would start the sentence by saying "I" and then mouthing the word *want* so that she would say it herself instead of relying on me to do it. As time went on, I'd repeat the same with the word *I*. Once she got the hang of how to put sentences together, her verbal abilities really took off!! It was these moments that always reminded me why I was so determined to stay the course. I used to imagine what it would be like to have an actual conversation with Danielle, and although it came in short portions here and there at the start, it was happening. What a joy it was to watch her blossom into this beautiful young girl who

94

had an unbelievable appreciation for life, not to mention she had the most contagious laugh I'd ever heard.

The past couple of years held more than their share of great accomplishments as well as numerous defeats. There were times I would have to stop and evaluate myself as to whether I was an incredibly positive and determined woman or if I had actually crossed over to the wonderful world of "I feel pretty?" But no matter my reality, incredible strides had been made, and I was more than elated not only about all that had been done but where Danielle was headed.

There's a saying that has been an encouragement to me for years. It goes like this: "You don't have to have it all figured out to move forward!" To that, I can only say, amen!

CHAPTER 17

SOCCER SILLIES

To choose hope, is to choose life!
—Chicko N. Okazaki

The numerous lessons I was privy to during these last two years seemed to far exceed a lifetime of previous ones. Some were empowering, while others left me devastated and longing for a simpler way through this unending battle. It was wonderful having Danielle communicating her wants and needs on a more engaging level, but realistically, we still weren't out of the woods. Although I greatly appreciated every milestone (big or small) that she had come through, it was more than obvious that our journey wasn't over, the mere fact that she still did her best work in a one-on-one setting was still a valid concern. Danielle proved she could learn in a social setting, but her greatest success was still one-on-one. So, my to-do list was getting quite lengthy. There were lines to be drawn, dots to connect, schedules to make, and boundaries (which changed daily) to be established, not to mention that making dinner and bedtime routines were not yet even in the mix.

This chaotic new agenda gave way to a whole new look for me that was far from impressive—crazy hair (contained only by hair ties and clips), no makeup, and moments of sheer panic when I couldn't find the deodorant.

(However, brushing my teeth was a priority, and my Tic Tacs were always conveniently close at hand.)

A full schedule didn't exactly allow me to get everything done as I would have liked to, although I was up early and consistently stayed up late. No matter what my earlier efforts of preparation were, it appeared that getting through some days was literally like trying to walk a straight line after an all-night drinking binge. Even a simple grocery run could be disastrous. Then, every once in a blue moon, I'd come across a day when everything would somehow just fall into place, giving me the illusion that I was in control of things—the operative word here being *illusion*.

My close friend Debbie had encouraged me to get my girls involved in soccer, stating it was great social exposure that would benefit them both, especially if they were on the same team. So, acting on her advice (because, of course, I wasn't busy enough), I signed both Ashley and Danielle up. I really enjoyed watching them learn to play a sport, navigating the ball up and down the field and more, not to mention all the social exposure that was happening. It was good advice, to say the least.

However, upon arriving at the field one afternoon about a month after they started playing, I was approached by the coach. He asked me if I had a moment to speak with him. He spoke in that tone that immediately puts a parent in Please-God-make-me-invisible mode. Although on the hesitant side, I agreed and stood somberly to hear what I was sure to be a one-sided conversation. Sadly, I was not disappointed. He told me that although Ashley showed great promise with her soccer abilities, she needed to leave her Barbies at home because the sidelines were turning into a Barbie playhouse. He went on further to inform me that Danielle (that very afternoon) just decided to walk off during practice and lie down in the grass at the end of the soccer field with her hands behind her head. When he inquired as to what she was doing, she simply said, "I'm taking a rest. I'll be back in a minute." He then told me quite candidly that my girls were *not* soccer player material and suggested I find a different sport to enroll them in. The truth of the matter was that Ashley only had the Barbies with her that day because it was show-and-tell at school, and

Danielle was the kind of kid that if she needed a break, she took one but would always politely ask first.

When I inquired as to whether she had asked his permission before walking away, he said, "Yeah, she asked, but I told her she could take one when I felt it was time!"

My only thought was: *Well, alrighty then.*

After he was done verbally tearing apart my children to my face, his body language stated that he felt very accomplished, as if to say, *what do you think of that?* He seemed to indicating with every fiber that my girls didn't fit the mold of true athletes (which, of course, he could clearly deduct at four and six years old)—probably not a good idea with a mom who's passionate about her children's success and sarcastic enough to let you know that you've just crossed some serious lines on that journey.

In all honesty, my first thought was to address the arrogance radiating from him. But I knew that he would only get further enjoyment from seeing me lose it, so after pausing briefly, I turned to him and softly stated that he was probably right.

My words seemed to strike a happy note in his ever-widening ego as he said, "Yeah, why's that?"

To which I promptly replied, "Did you know that it's a proven fact that good athletes excel with coaches who are encouraging and make it a practice of praising their players as opposed to cutting them down? Realistically, you don't fall into that category, so it's beside the point.

"The point here is that critiquing a player and criticizing her are two different concepts, and I would seriously encourage you learn the difference between them before this season really takes off and you risk losing all your players, as well as the games."

His momentary silence indicated I had somewhat leveled the playing field between us. In turning to leave, I calmly added that as soon as his son was done playing with my daughter's barbies, I'd have her put them back in her bag. With that, I softly smiled and bid him a good afternoon.

After gathering up my girls, we all went home where I fed, bathed, and tucked the kids into bed. Later, as I sat on the couch, I cried—not just because the coach's words hurt but because I knew that he represented the kind of people my girls would be up against throughout their lives. These people only see themselves and have no vision for others outside the circle of privileged individuals of their choosing.

I fought so many uphill battles day in and day out. It seemed like we would no sooner take a couple of steps forward when something would send us reeling twice as many steps backward. It was a very raw moment in the realm of reality but not anything I didn't believe God couldn't get us through. So, what was a brokenhearted mom to do but to cry it out, give the pieces to God, and thank Him that tomorrow was a new day?

CHAPTER 18

CHOICES

"You're such a strong and determined woman, Maggie. I really admire your courage."

I had heard these words many, many times as my children were growing up but for some reason found it hard to accept the compliments that came my way after Danielle was diagnosed. Naturally, I would always thank them for their kindness, but deep inside, I struggled desperately with their words of praise. It wasn't because I didn't appreciate what they said by any means; it just seemed to always hit a chord of discontent.

In all honesty, I had no idea why it made me so uncomfortable hearing their compliments, and I wasn't sure what to do about it. I was confused as to how I could problem-solve and come up with various solutions to my daughter's struggles, yet I couldn't figure out why receiving simple affirmation for a job well done was such an issue.

"This is so ridiculous!" I said while on the phone with a close friend one day. "It's like being mad at someone, but you have no idea what you're mad at!"

Further on into our conversation, she happened to say, "You're such a strong woman, Maggie. Danielle's blessed to have you as her mom!"

Normally, a statement like that would be followed by an, "Oh my gosh, thank you," or, "That's so nice of you!" Yet, I was silent, which was confirmation enough to us both that there was a deeper issue going on. It was like hammering a nail only to realize it was your thumb in the line of fire, immediately rendering you speechless and in pain. Her words hurt, but why? As we conversed a bit more, the topic shifted to the day it all began, which was in the doctor's office with the nurse who had given Danielle the double helping of the MMR shot.

Up until that point, I don't believe I was even aware that I had been carrying so much resentment. But as our conversation opened, it was like a dam at flood stage, surprising even me as out spilled some of the most agonizing tears and words I had expressed in a long time.

My friend was attempting to console me when I literally erupted, saying, "How could you possibly say I'm the strong one when Danielle is the one going through it all? Can't you see that I was the one who caused it in the first place?"

As more painful silence filled the air, everything momentarily seemed so ugly and hopeless, but as we began to separate things slowly and piece them back together, only then could I see a glimmer of hope for my aching heart. The truth was, it was not my fault, and I never could have predicted that the nurse would have injected her with the syringe a second time. I felt I had been very clear on asking for the doctor to be called in, but that was not her intentions. Although I didn't realize it at the time, I had silently chosen to absorb all the blame, hence allowing anger a stronghold in my heart and mind.

As a mom who's always been crazy about her children, the mere thought of hindering any of their hopes and dreams before they even had a chance to dream them tore me apart from the inside out. I wanted nothing more for Danielle than to have every chance in life that her sisters had, and with the realization that those chances might not be what they were before the doctor's visit, it literally brought me to my knees, all the while shattering me from within.

I desperately began to seek God about how to remove this silent, angry mountain that had been trying to take up residence in my heart. My friend encouraged me to forgive the nurse, the doctor, and anyone else who had to do with that day (including myself). To be honest, I didn't want to forgive anyone! I mean, why should I? They hurt my family, but most importantly, they hurt my child! It was here, however, that I learned one of the most important lessons of my life, which was that when you choose to let go of the anger you're holding toward someone else, you become better equipped to move on with things in your own life.

Forgiveness isn't necessarily about freeing the guilty party. It's about freeing yourself. When I asked God to help me forgive all involved that day, I found a freedom that I had no idea existed and was able to move out of the place I had been stuck in since things began. I remember a couple weeks later being out with a friend and realizing that I was actually laughing out loud, which, of course, made me laugh even harder. I literally felt like a hard drive that had been defragged—more room, more freedom. It was a win, win situation in my eyes.

I've candidly shared this part of my story because many of you reading this book are possibly experiencing the same frustration that I've faced and more. Although everybody's journey is different, each one is still just as important. I want to encourage you to stay the course. No matter how upside down things look all around you or whatever has been said or done, stay the course. I can say without reservation that forgiveness in every sense of the word is a worthwhile venture. There's only unwanted pain to lose and a lifetime of peace to gain.

If you have found yourself in a similar situation, let me encourage your heart by saying that God knows and cares deeply about everything you and your family are going through! He will meet you in the darkest moments and walk hand in hand with you through the storm.

Helen Keller, one of the strongest women in history, penned these powerful words years ago: "Character cannot be developed in ease and quiet. Only through experience of trial and suffering can the soul be strengthened, ambition inspired, and success achieved."

CHAPTER 19

BROKEN WINGS

Life, without a doubt, holds its little surprises. Some are not as welcomed, while others are just what the doctor ordered. The summer after I learned to forgive myself, I happened to be in my kitchen washing dishes one day, and Danielle (now five) stood next to me casually leaning her head on my leg. She seemed so content I almost forgot she was there until I turned to get something off the counter behind me.

At that point, I looked down and saw her puppy-dog eyes staring directly into mine and immediately felt my heart melting like putty on a stove. With one simple little question, she managed to finish me off by asking, "Mommy, why do you love me?" The absolute sincerity and innocence of what she had asked struck a chord so deep I almost burst into tears on the spot. Instead, I quietly dried my hands-on a nearby hand towel and grabbed a small kitchen stool to sit on as I swept my little angel up and gently sat her onto my lap. As I peered into those trusting little eyes, I knew I had her undivided attention, and she was totally aware that she had mine.

I felt I needed to use my best storytelling abilities to let my baby girl know that she was loved beyond words, and as I opened my mouth, a story as sweet and tender as her escaped from my heart to my lips.

I painted a simple but real-life picture of Jesus anxiously walking back and forth in heaven with this beautiful baby girl, asking, "Who will take this child? Is there anyone who will take her home and love her?"

Danielle immediately chimed in and asked, "Why didn't anyone want her, Mommy?"

To which I replied, "I'm so glad you asked! You see, the only problem with this little angel is that she had a broken wing, which, of course, was why no one wanted her in the first place. But Jesus wants every child to have a loving home, so he takes extra care as to who he gives his little angels to.

"So, in the middle of Jesus walking back and forth, He turned around and saw Mommy and Daddy jumping up and down like crazy people, waving their hands back and forth yelling 'We want her! We want her! *Please* ... Can we have her?'"

Danielle laughed hysterically at the thought of her mom and dad jumping around, especially since I was eagerly acting it all out.

I continued, "Jesus, being extremely excited He had found a home for you, agreed to let us have you and placed you in Mommy's tummy to bless us."

She looked satisfied and content for a moment, and then slowly, a perplexed look came across her face as she asked, "So what happened to my broken wing?"

I had to laugh as I explained to her that she'd asked a wonderful question. "The fact is Jesus has the best super glue in the world, so He put a little bit on your wing before He gave you to us, and by the time you were born, no one could even tell it was broke at all!"

She seemed quite content after that as I kissed her on the forehead and scooted her off to the playroom where her sister was. I was elated beyond words that she was able to engage in a conversation of this level. Every time a moment like this came along, I felt blessed and encouraged at the same time. *Hope* had been a word I had clung to, refusing to let go even in the face of others telling me to give up, and it was times like these that reminded me why I chose to stand my ground and even more grateful that God was standing with me!

CHAPTER 20

EAGLES

You can't go back and change the beginning, but you can start where you are and change the ending!

—Author unknown

Sometime around the beginning of January 2000, Janis from Lighthouse Services had moved on to another family, and I decided at that point it was time we moved on as well. So, as one journey ended, another had begun with The Children's Center located just a couple of towns away. I had done some research ahead of time on the center which helped reassure my heart that these were the people I wanted working with my daughter.

The minute Anna (the district supervisor) and Jasmine (the home-based worker) walked in to have their first meeting with our family, it was more than obvious that I had made the best choice for my child. They were friendly, knowledgeable, and super easy to talk to. They always kept us updated with Danielle's progress, as well as where they were headed next in her program, and I greatly appreciated them.

On March 3, 2000, Anna and Jasmine both went to Danielle's elementary school to observe her in the classroom, and it went better than I had anticipated. Danielle came home on the school bus arriving about ten minutes before they did, and as she walked through the door, she kind of sauntered past me asking if I would please make her some chocolate milk and snuggle her up on the couch. I couldn't help but laugh at the moment that in some ways mirrored a teenager coming home from college and asking, "Hey, Mom, would you mind doing my laundry, and by the way, what's for dinner?" Too funny! So just as I got Danielle settled on the couch, Anna and Jasmine arrived, and we assembled in the kitchen to discuss how the observation at school went.

I was elated when they told me that Danielle was doing amazing—definitely sweet words to my heart. They said that they deliberately compared her to the other children in the classroom who did not carry a diagnosis, and she actually came out on top. They also told me the teacher had to redirect her for whispering and giggling to a classmate during circle time. (I don't promote disobedience in the classroom but seeing as it was her first sign of independence, I let it slide!)

The next afternoon while at the supermarket I had all three girls with me. As we were walking up and down the aisles, there were several coupon dispensers stationed randomly and conveniently at a child's height. So, as we made our way through the store, Ashley and Danielle were busy trying their best to deplete the dispensers of their coupons (or, in their eyes, money). I told them they had enough money and needed to leave the rest for others who didn't have as much. So, without hesitation, Danielle immediately turned to an older couple who had been walking behind us and said, "Excuse me. Here's a couple of bucks so you can go buy yourself something!" and walked back to stand next to me.

I was almost laughing out loud as the elderly gentleman turned to his wife and exclaimed, "I've always wished that someone would walk up and give me money!"

The exact moment Danielle's personality had begun to blossom had eluded me, but I would find myself so many times smiling at the different little things that she would randomly say or do, and I was in awe of what God was doing in her little life.

March 23, 2000 was a pretty hectic day as another neurological appointment for Danielle was set for six o'clock that night. The office was also about an hour away, which meant after the kids got out of school, I had to make sure they ate dinner and bathed before we left because we wouldn't be getting home until around nine o'clock or later, and it was a school night.

As we arrived and the appointment got underway, everything seemed to be going extremely well. The neurologist was very impressed with Danielle's accomplishments. As she received the gathered information from various areas such as school, home, and The Child Center, she seemed to be more than intrigued by her progress. Dr. Maddie said she was truly happy with her and that she wanted to extend our next visit to a year out instead of six months. There were still some valid concerns, but this visit let me know that we were definitely on the right road with her progress. Two weeks later, the doctor's evaluation came in:

> Danielle is a very pretty, blonde haired little girl who comes readily to the examining room with her parents. Her height is at 41-1/2 inches, her weight is 34-1/2 pounds. Her general physical examination is unremarkable and there are no obvious dysmorphic features.
>
> Motorically, she continues to be a very low tone child with hypermobility of the joints throughout.
>
> In summary, Danielle is now a 5-year-old child, who has been carrying a diagnosis of Pervasive Developmental Disorder – Not Otherwise Specified (PDD-NOS). Danielle has continued to make exceptional progress, not only demonstrated by her presence here in the office, but also verified by classroom teachers, therapists, and parents. Motorically, she appears to be more able and is now socially, language-wise, quite competent. Occasionally there remains some remnants of language

disabilities to the extent that when asked a question, she has a tendency to turn away in an attempt to answer you. She does not always answer the question in a demand situation. It is difficult to know how much of this relates to being 5 years old and how much of this relates to her underlying diagnosis. Certainly, both may be at play here. Nonetheless, Danielle will require continual monitoring in regard to any possible language problems in the near future.

I was so excited when I read this evaluation that I immediately hit my knees, thanking God over and over for His mercies in my daughter's life as well as mine. A friend of mine sent me this story shortly after Danielle was diagnosed, and I remember crying after reading it because I wanted so much for her to be above the storm like this eagle. I somehow misplaced it over time and stumbled upon it just days after this new evaluation arrived in the mail.

Eagles in a Storm

Did you know that an eagle knows when a storm is approaching long before it breaks? The eagle will fly to some high spot and wait for the winds to come. When the storm hits, it sets its wings so that the wind will pick it up and lift it above the storm. While the storm rages below, the eagle is soaring above it.

The eagle does not escape the storm. It simply uses the storm to lift it higher. It rises on the winds that bring the storm.

It was a wonderful reminder to me that it's not the burdens of life that weigh us down; it's how we handle them. The Bible says, "Those who hope in the Lord will renew their strength. They will soar on wings like eagles" (Is. 40:31).

CHAPTER **21**

LITTLE BUTTERFLY

Perhaps the butterfly is proof that you can go through a great deal of darkness yet become something beautiful.

—TobyMac, #Speak life

As the next year began to unfold, I saw my Danielle blossom from this tiny, timid caterpillar into a beautiful little butterfly. Her language and other social aspects were right where they needed to be, and I don't think I could have asked God for more as a mom. Anna and Jasmine worked extremely hard with Danielle and, in the process, became a part of our forever family.

I'll never forget the day Anna came for her monthly home assessment and stated that Danielle was doing so well that she would only need The Children's Center's services till the end of the summertime. Her words left me momentarily speechless, So many wonderful reports were coming back from every direction I could hardly keep track of them all, and by the time we saw the neurologist almost a year later, Danielle was literally on target as an almost-six-year-old and maybe even a bit ahead of her peers.

The only odd behavior I observed from Danielle during that year was that her hand preference had gone from left-handed to right. As she was drawing at the kitchen counter one afternoon, I passed by and saw her reach across with her right hand to grab a crayon on her left side. I paused for a moment to watch her a bit closer, and sure enough, she was doing everything right-handed. I purposely put a crayon in her left hand to see what she would do, and she immediately switched it to her right hand and continued drawing as if that's what she had done from the start. I spoke to The Children's Center as well as her teachers, and they said that they too noticed a change in her hand dominance, which had seemed to transpire rather quickly over the last couple of months. So we all agreed that it would be a great question for Dr. Maddie at the next appointment since it was just a few days out.

February 1, 2001 was probably the most memorable appointment I had gone to since everything had begun. As we walked in, we were kindly greeted by Dr. Maddie. She was this calm, confident, and well poised little grandmother-type woman who needed no introductions. She was so well known that when others held conferences on autism, they would literally footnote her while speaking to great crowds. I thanked God often for allowing her to be Danielle's neurologist throughout this process because she was unmistakably a wise and well-seasoned professional.

While at her office that night, we talked nonstop about Danielle's accomplishments and how wonderful she looked in every area. Dr. Maddie Looked at me and said, "Nice job, Momma!"

Although I was ecstatic and beaming with pride, my first words to her were, "I can't take any credit until I first give God the glory."

To which, she immediately replied, "I would too!"

We both sat there with grateful grins on our faces, and for a moment, it almost felt like we were at Grandma's house waiting for someone to pass around the homemade cookies and warm milk. She always put you at ease.

I shared our concerns about how Danielle's hand dominance had changed during the past couple months, and she said she could order up some detailed evaluations and do a series of CAT scans on her brain if that's what

I wanted. Even then, they might come back inconclusive and provide no answers. Because Danielle was functioning so well in school and otherwise, she said she wasn't really that concerned at that time, so we kind of put it on the shelf and moved on.

As our conversation briefly paused, I took the opportunity to ask her another question that had been on my mind for months. So, I said, "Excuse me, Dr. Maddie, but would you mind if I ask you a random question?"

Her response was kind yet quick as she said, "Yes, dear? What is it?"

Although I felt a bit hesitant, I leaned forward and said, "Does anyone with autism ever actually lose their diagnoses? I mean, she's doing so well, and I was just wondering if it could happen at some point is all."

Her demeanor changed from lighthearted to being instantly serious as she reached for the manila folder that was sitting on the little table in front of her. After picking it up, she simply said, "Hmmm ... Well, let's see where we are, why don't we."

Dr. Maddie was not the kind of person you rushed or pushed into making any kind of a quick decision ... ever. She took her time, and that was that. I must have sat there no less than five to ten minutes while she thumbed through all the paperwork in the folder, and when she was thoroughly satisfied, she closed the folder and gently laid it on the table in front of her. Then, with only a slight hesitation, she slowly sat back in her chair as though she were in deep thought and asked, "Does anyone ever tell you that your daughter was *misdiagnosed*?"

My response was immediate. "All the time. Why?"

She reached for the folder again, looked it over for another minute or two, and said, "Tell them I said they were wrong!" And with her next words, she set my heart soaring at a level I had never known before as she said, "And as of this moment, her diagnosis is lifted!"

It is a moment that will forever be etched in my mind.

When the appointment was over, we said our goodbyes and walked outside to the parking lot. Everything seemed so surreal to me. The stars were brighter, the air smelled fresher, and my Danielle, who just moments before had been handed a second chance at life, was smiling and holding my hand. I was literally breathless with excitement! As we began our journey home, I glanced in the back seat briefly only to see Danielle and Ashley leaning on each other soundly sleeping and knew beyond a doubt that God had given me a very precious gift.

The only thing running through my mind was *She's normal! She's normal! Oh, God, thank you for hearing my prayers!*

I felt as victorious as David the day he killed Goliath with a tiny stone that was guided by a *big God*!

The last evaluation came in just a week later.

> Danielle Weathersby is now a 6-year-old child who has carried a diagnosis of Pervasive Developmental Disorder – Not Otherwise Specified. Danielle was last seen for a neurological consultation almost a year ago (3/23/00) and returns today for repeat consultation in the company of her parents, her older sister, Ashley, and her younger sister, Shannon.
>
> Mrs. Weathersby brings with her several pieces of Danielle's work from school. At this present time, she is enrolled in an inclusion kindergarten housed within their Public-School District. This particular program meets daily and contains about 15 children. Danielle carries an educational plan, that provides her with one half hour per month of occupational therapy.
>
> Danielle continues to receive four hours of classroom observation and consultation designed to monitor her learning style and to ensure that Danielle is receiving appropriate services given her underlying diagnosis. So far

however she seems to be doing extremely well. Danielle's schoolwork shows her ability to write, her coloring has improved, and she has developed some sight word vocabulary and she is beginning to read and understand number concepts. Her play skills have expanded, and she is showing some improved pretend play as well as interactions with other children, including her siblings.

On examination today, Danielle's height is 48 inches and her weight is 38 pounds. She's a very cute, blonde haired little girl with good eye contact, who seems to be quite verbal and has no trouble interacting with either of her siblings or "holding her own."

In summary, Danielle Weathersby is now nearly a 6-year-old child, who has been carrying a diagnosis of Pervasive Developmental Disorder – Not Otherwise Specified (PDD-NOS). Danielle has definitely made incredible progress over the past several years and currently, **no longer fulfills the criteria for Pervasive Developmental Disorder in any category.** Although I feel it's too soon to tell whether her previous symptoms will have any impact on her ability to achieve academically without any difficulty, the signs so far indicate that she is a bright little girl who seems to be keeping up at this point.

On the heels of this *amazing* evaluation, Anna and Jasmine handed me their last home-based quarterly report just a couple days later.

Danielle worked extremely well during the final quarter. She was able to achieve eight annual objectives. These objectives were:

1. Putting a six-step sequence in order and telling about them.

2. Answering "who," "what," "when," and/or "where" questions.

3. Identifying objects in and out of view when given a description of the object.

4. Describing and identifying irregularities in pictures.

5. Receptively identifying and expressively labeling numbers 1-10.

6. Copying her name from a model with 2 or fewer prompts.

7. Matching 5 written words to objects.

8. Answering questions about a story.

Also, Danielle is progressing with seven of her objectives. These objectives will continue to be worked on and/or maintained in the future. During this IEP period (Individualized Educational Plan), Danielle has demonstrated incredible understanding and development of her skills. This understanding and development can be observed at home, in school, and in her ability to generalize her skills. She has created positive relationships with her peers and teachers and has interacted appropriately with each. **Danielle is a friendly and caring little girl who has a bright future ahead of her!

While on my knees that night, I could only softly cry tears of joy and appreciation for all that God had done, and with a full heart and tired eyes, I whispered to Jesus, "My cup runneth over!"

CHAPTER 22

THE DANCE

Life isn't about waiting for the storm to pass. It's about learning to dance in the rain!

So many nights I had spent praying desperately for God to just heal Danielle, yet nothing happened. Wasn't I sincere enough? Didn't He care? So many tough but important lessons throughout those tear-stained years, yet I learned an important life lesson, which was just because God doesn't answer our prayers immediately in our designated time frame, it doesn't mean He didn't hear us.

There are times He asks us to wait, not because He doesn't care what's happening but because He's giving us an opportunity to *trust Him in the middle of the storm*. Looking back, I can see so many places where He not only carried me but strengthened me in the process. Since our journey began, God's presented me with one opportunity after another to share my daughter's story with hurting families who were just beginning theirs. I've been both humbled and blessed to be a part of encouraging and inspiring others during their tough times, realizing that God's plans are so much more fulfilling.

There was a popular song on the radio called "I Hope You Dance" written by Lee Ann Womack. Every time I heard it play, I would pick my girls up one by one and dance around the room, all the while laughing and singing. The day after the last evaluation had arrived in the mail, as the song began to play, we danced around the room with more purpose and passion than we had ever done.

The lyrics are beautiful:

> I hope you never lose your sense of wonder
> You get your fill to eat but always keep that hunger,
> May you never take one single breath for granted,
> God forbid love ever leave you empty-handed.
> I hope you still feel small when you stand beside the ocean,
> Whenever one door closes, I hope one more opens,
> I hope you dance
> I hope you dance!

The lyrics in this song were not just mere words; they were my heart's prayer! I wanted all my girls—not just Danielle—to live life to the fullest! I wanted them to dream big dreams, achieve all they desire to achieve, and, most importantly, to love and be loved in return. I think just realizing that these opportunities were now in her hands as well was enough to encourage my heart to eternity and back.

That night in my journal I wrote:

> I am incredibly grateful and humbled to you God, for giving me blessings beyond what my heart can contain. I cried for the storm to stop, but instead you held my hand and taught me to dance in the rain! Your love is unconditional, and I will forever give you the glory for this journey through autism!

EPILOGUE

Danielle continues to grow and achieve her goals in every facet of life. When she was in fifth grade, she was given an assignment in school in which she had to write about a person in her family who was her hero and give at two reasons why.

This is what Danielle wrote:

> My hero in my life would be my mom. I admire her a lot. My mom, to me, is the most loving person I have ever met. She is fun to be around and is always nice. And there are so many reasons why I admire her so much. But I will give the two most important reasons why she's my hero and why admire her so much.
>
> The first reason is because she's always been there for me no matter what. Through the good and through the bad. She is always there for me when I am sick or feeling down. My mom is the person who gets me through my bad days and takes care of me when I am sick.
>
> The second reason why my mom is my hero is because she would do just about anything to make me happy. My mom has provided me with everything I could possibly ask for. She makes me lunch, buys food, buys me games and toys, and all kinds of stuff. But yet I don't say thank

you all the time but, still she doesn't mind. And that makes me feel like she really loves me.

I would do anything for my mom. And I love her very much! Those are my two main reasons why my mom is my hero and why I admire her a lot!

By Danielle Weathersby

My thoughts? Coolest paper I've ever read, but truth be known, she's my hero. Watching God mold, shape, and blossom this little angel into the beautiful young woman she is today has been one of my greatest blessings. The lessons I was privy to were many, and I am immensely proud of my Danielle in every way. Today she is the epitome of a successful woman whose accomplishments are many. Although she and God are still writing her story, my heart will forever remain in awe not because of how far she's come but because of how far she's going.

> *You're off to great places! Today is your day! Your*
> *mountain is waiting, so get on your way!*
> —Dr. Seuss

THE FOLLOWING ARE
VARIOUS EVALUATION'S

Early Intervention:
July 7-22, 1997

Danielle was a full-term baby weighed 8lbs 10oz. at birth. She did not require any special medication attention while in the hospital at birth. Early medical history is excellent with the exception of the diagnosis of Henoch Schonlum Syndrome Purprick in June 1996 which may have been caused by the MMR vaccine.

Danielle demonstrated skills at the 24-month level in gross motor and adaptive with skills in personal-social, language, cognition, and fine motor significantly below age level. Her limited interest in many of the items as well as her limited social interactions with the play facilitator seem to be impacting on her developmental progress. I recommend that Danielle receive Early Intervention services to help her developmental progress with an emphasis on language and social skills.

Danielle demonstrated personal-social skills significantly below age level. She was difficult for the play facilitator to engage in activities, showing a limited interest in many of the activities presented to her during the assessment period. She briefly engaged in play with manipulative tasks such as stacking blocks and placing pegs in the peg board. She was also observed to engage in repetitive play behaviors such as play with a flashlight. Danielle didn't respond to play facilitator's requests. She seemed to limit her interactions and avoid eye contact with others. Danielle was observed to express a wide range of feelings, smiling when happy and crying or fussing when upset. She seemed to be easily frustrated when directed to an activity or when she wasn't given something she was asking for.

Danielle demonstrated adaptive skills at the 24-month level. Her mother expressed that she eats a variety of foods and at this point doesn't seem to have any difficulty chewing or swallowing. She finger feeds herself and uses a spoon to eat. Her mother also reported that she drinks from a sippie cup.

Danielle demonstrated gross motor skills at the 24-27-month level. She demonstrated a variety of play positions, sitting, squatting, standing and transitioned easily from one position to another position. She walked and ran well, maintaining balance when starting, turning, and stopping. Her mother said that she can walk up and down stairs if she's holding someone's hand. She was also observed to jump in place. Danielle threw a ball forward, but she was not observed to kick a ball.

Danielle demonstrated fine motor skills solidly at the 15-month level with a scattering of skills up to the 23-month level. Danielle used a variety of grasps on objects, using a raking motion and an inferior pincer grasp on tiny objects such as a cheerio and a radial digital grasp on small objects such as an inch cube. She demonstrated an accurate release of object, stacking six-inch cubes and placing half inch pegs in a peg board. Danielle didn't attempt to complete a three-piece form board. Nor did she attempt to imitate any strokes.

Danielle's language comprehension abilities were estimated to be at the 11-month level. She was observed to turn her head to locate the source of a novel sound. She inconsistently looked up in response to her name being called. Danielle's mother reported that Danielle will sometimes follow directions accompanied by gestural cues (e.g., Give me the baby.) and that there are specific phrases that she understands (e.g., Let's go get a pop. Let's go take a bath. Let's go outside.) Danielle's eye contact with the examiner was fleeting and she was not observed to point to body parts on herself or others or to point to objects or pictures of objects upon request. Danielle's mother also reported that Danielle is not interested in looking at picture books but will quickly flip through the pictures but that she loves watching animated videos on television.

Danielle's language expression abilities were judged to be at the 15-month level. Danielle communicated wants and needs by handing a toy back to the examiner to activate. This gesture was at times accompanied by vocalizations. At home, Danielle's mother reported that Danielle will take mom's hand and walk her toward what she wants, or she will attempt to get desired object on her own. She used "no-no" meaningfully several times during this assessment and Danielle's mother reported that in the past 3 months Danielle has also acquired "mama," moo/for cow, and "uh-oh." She reported that Danielle was saying "mama and dada" at six months and then stopped at 14 months after the MMR shot. During this assessment Danielle imitated "uh/for up," "ss/for yes" in imitation of the play facilitator.

Danielle demonstrated cognitive skills at the 12-15-month level. She engaged in some relational play such as stacking blocks and placing rings on a stack. Danielle did not engage in any symbolic play activities either directed toward herself or a doll. In the area of memory, she found a toy hidden under several covers, but she became frustrated when the toy was hidden under multiple covers. In the area of problem solving, Danielle inverted a container to obtain an object and nested four containers. Her mother reported that she will move a chair to obtain an object that is out of reach. Danielle was difficult to engage in many of the activities but once engaged she persisted with a task on her own, occasionally gesturing to the play facilitator for assistance.

Danielle's mother did not report any concerns for her vision or hearing.

First Homebased Evaluation:
September 1997

OBJECTIVE: (What you ultimately want her to be able to do.)

BASELINE: (Where she began in her performance of a certain goal.)

This is for September 1997:

(1) Objective: **Eye Contact.** In response to "Danielle, look at me" while sitting in chairs facing each other.

Baseline: 0%

(2) Objective: **Object Imitation.** Imitating an action with an object when presented with a teacher's model across a variety of materials.

Baseline: Unreliable data with familiar materials and action seemingly imitative but wouldn't imitate an alternative response with same materials.

(3) Objective: **Gross Motor Imitation.**

Baseline: 0%

(4) Objective: **Vocal Imitation.**

Baseline: Unreliable Data

(5) Objective: **Knowing Body Parts.**

Baseline: 0%

(6) Objective: **To answer Yes/No – In response to, do you want this?**

Baseline: 0%

(7) Objective: **Grapho-Motor Imitation – Pre-writing skills.**

Baseline: 0%

(8) Objective: **Expressive Language – In response to, what is this?**

Baseline: 0%

(9) Objective: **Requests – Initiates requests for desired objects or activities.**

Baseline: 100% using vocal approximations for bubbles, cookie, Play-Doh, and sock.

(10) Objective: **One Step Directions.**

Baseline: 0%

Homebased Evaluation:
June 23, 1998

Presently, Danielle will make eye contact when given the instruction, "Look at me," 90% of the time. Eye contact is also consistent when addressing Danielle by name. Danielle is continuously working on staying with an activity until the command, "All done," is given.

Danielle is currently working on block structures with four blocks. She is successful 70% of the time with full verbal prompts.

Danielle is currently working on diagonal lines, smile faces, and tracing a circle. She is successful 90% of the time when given light wrist support.

Danielle has currently mastered her name, age, her sister's name, hair color, eye color, town, mother's name, how are you? and her favorite drink. Danielle is currently working on her last name, school's name, and her teachers' names.

Danielle is presently working on "I see a ___." She is given picture cues as a prompt and is successful 90% of the time.

Danielle has mastered on, in, under, next to, and on top. Danielle will be introduced to "in front of" this week.

Danielle has learned each body part. However, she is working on being accurate when several body parts are asked at a session. She is successful 70% of the time.

Danielle has learned eight shapes. She is successful 80% of the time.

Danielle has mastered numbers one and two. She has recently been introduced to the number three. It is presently being modeled.

Danielle has mastered the upper-case letters. She is working on the lower-case. She has mastered a, b, c, d, e, and f.

Mastered Programs:

1. Yes/No questions
2. Colors
3. Emotions (Happy, sad, angry, silly, surprised, tired, and scared)
4. Action words

Homebased Evaluation:
July 22, 1998

Presently, Danielle will make eye contact when given the instruction, "Look at me," 90% of the time. Eye contact is also consistent when addressing Danielle by name. Danielle is continuously working on staying with an activity until the command, "All done," is given.

Danielle is currently working on block structures with four blocks. She is successful 80% of the time.

Simple line drawings/Tracing: Danielle is currently working on diagonal lines, smile faces, and tracing a square. She is successful 90% of the time when given light wrist support.

Danielle is currently successful 80% of the time. The first action is completed in her chair, while the second action is completed out of her chair.

Danielle is successful 80% of the time with two objects.

Danielle is currently working on community service people. Such as a fireman, doctor, mailman, teacher, and a hairdresser.

Danielle has currently mastered her name, age, her sister's name, hair color, eye color, town, mother's name, how are you? favorite drink, father's name, school's name, and her last name. She is currently working on her teacher's name.

Danielle is presently working on "I see a____ and a ____." She is given picture cues as a prompt and is successful 90% of the time.

Danielle has mastered on, in, under, next to, and on top. Danielle will be introduced to "in front of" this week.

Danielle has mastered big/little, up/down, fast/slow, open/closed, and empty/full. She is working on near/far and is successful 60% of the time.

Danielle is successful 80% of the time with ten combinations. Such as, "why do you smile?" _____ "I am happy." "What do you do if your happy?" _____ "I smile."

Danielle is currently working on eyes, nose, and ears. She is successful 70% of the time.

Danielle can identify the numbers 1, 4, 5, 6, and 8. She is working on counting objects up to five and pointing to each object as she counts. Danielle is able to count to thirteen independently.

Danielle has mastered the upper-case letters. She is working on lower-case. She can identify about 80%.

Danielle has mastered items that are the same. She is working on different and is successful 70% of the time.

Danielle is currently working on more and is successful 50% of the time.

Mastered Programs:

1. Yes/No Questions
2. Colors
3. Emotions (Happy, Sad, Angry, Silly, Surprised, Tired and Scared).
4. Action words
5. Shapes
6. Body Parts

Homebased Evaluation:
September 8, 1998

Presently, Danielle will make eye contact when given the instruction, "Look at me," 90% of the time. Eye contact is also consistent when addressing Danielle by name. Danielle is continuously working on staying with an activity until the command, "All done," is given.

Danielle is currently working on block structures with six blocks. She is successful 40% of the time.

Danielle is currently working on shapes, stick figures, and creating a house. She is successful 90% of the time when given light wrist support.

Danielle is currently successful 20% of the time. When the actions are modeled, Danielle is successful 70% of the time.

Danielle is successful 80% of the time with four objects.

Danielle has currently mastered her name, age, her sister's name, hair color, eye color, town, mother's name, How are you?, Favorite drink, favorite food, favorite t.v. show, favorite toy, father's name, school's name, and her last name. She is currently working on her teachers' names.

Danielle has mastered on, in, under, next to, on top, and in front of. Danielle will be introduced to "Between" this week.

Danielle has mastered big/little, up/down, fast/slow, open/closed, and empty/full, and near/far. She is working on forward/backward and is successful 70% of the time.

Danielle is currently working on eyes, nose, and ears. She is successful 90% of the time when asked "What are your eyes for, nose for, and ears for?" Danielle is working on, "What do you see with, hear with, and smell with?" She is successful 50% of the time.

Danielle locates items with specific attributes and answers related questions correctly 70% of the time. Such as, "What did you find?" and "Where did you find it?"

Danielle has been introduced to a cup and a pencil. She is correct 10% of the time.

Danielle can identify the numbers 1-9 80% of the time. She is working on counting objects up to ten and pointing to each object as she counts. Danielle is able to count to sixteen independently.

Danielle has mastered the upper-case letters. She is working on lower-case. She can identify about 90%.

Colors and objects are randomly shown, and Danielle is correct 70% with a partial verbal prompt.

Danielle is successful 90% of the time.

With two objects or colors, Danielle is correct 70% of the time with a partial verbal prompt.

Danielle is working on cutting a marked line. She needs adult to hold the paper.

Mastered Programs:

1. Yes/No Questions
2. Colors
3. Emotions (Happy, Sad, Angry, Silly, Surprised, Tired, and Scared)
4. Action words
5. Shapes
6. Body Parts
7. Why/If Questions (Why do you smile? ____ I am Happy. What do you do of your happy? ____ I smile.)
8. Pretending (actions, animals, and community leaders)
9. Two-step instructions

Homebased Evaluation:
October 30, 1998

Presently working on building structures with 7 blocks and is successful 75% of the time. This month she began tracing the upper-case alphabet and is making excellent progress, with light physical guidance can trace lines 95%, independently 25%.

Danielle is working on 3-step directions and is successful 80% of the time. Also, Danielle is working on "What's missing" with four objects and is successful 90% of the time.

Danielle is very busy working on personal questions prepositions, attributes, function of body part, and function of objects. She's doing very well, and some program changes will be put in place next week.

Danielle just started cutting horizontal and vertical lines with holding the paper alone. She's also working on tracing the upper-case alphabet as well as identifying her first and last name and numbers 1-20 receptively and expressively.

Homebased Evaluation:

November 30, 1998

A program change was implemented on 11/6/98 changing block imitation from 7 blocks to 8. At this time Danielle can independently imitate building with 8 blocks 90% of the time.

Danielle continues to work on increasing her expressive skills in the area of #'s 11-20, first and last name, personal questions, function of objects, and body parts.

11-20 is 70% independent (ind.) First name 85% individual, last name – 100%, Personal Quest – 95%, function of objects 95%, and function of body parts is 85% of the time. We are working on generalization in every area.

Danielle is increasing her receptive numbers 11-20 skills to 85%, first and last name receptive game that was introduced this month is now at mastery level. Danielle continues to follow three-step directions 75% of the time. This activity often depends on her level of compliance for the day. The "what's missing" game is now being played with 5 items, as of 11/20/98, and is at 70%.

Danielle began cutting horizontal/vertical lines early this month holding the paper independently. She has almost mastered this task and will introduce cutting shapes in December.

Danielle is working on tracing the alphabet and does fairly well. She can trace the lines an average of 45% of the time by herself and 100% of the time with light physical guidance.

Neurological Evaluation:
February 13, 1998

Danielle is a 35-month-old girl with a previous diagnosis of Pervasive Developmental Disorder who has made rather significant gains in social development and language development skills since her last appointment here. She, however, continues to display impairment in the areas of her social and language functions, thus continuing to meet criteria for a diagnosis of PDD – Not Otherwise Specified. It is this examiner's impression that her rather remarkable gains thus far are largely due to the intensity of therapeutic and educational services that she has been receiving as well as significant commitment on her Mother's behalf to further foster and carry over educational and behavioral strategies at home. At this Juncture, she is preparing to transition into a preschool setting, and it is imperative that appropriate services be fully implemented in order to make this transition a successful one and continue to foster her positive developmental course.

Neurological Evaluation:
July 24, 1998

Danielle Weathersby is a now 3 year 4-month-old child with a diagnosis of Pervasive developmental Disorder – Not Otherwise Specified. She continues to make excellent gains, both socially and in language, as well as in pretend play skills. Motorically, she's gaining as well. This fall, it's expected that she will enter into a small integrated preschool program but will continue to receive speech and language support within the context of this program.

Although Danielle has made excellent gains, it should be noted that children at this level have skills which are still incredibly fragile. Failure to continue to provide the support systems which have allowed them to make these gains, runs the substantial risk of significant regression during this time. Therefore, every effort should be made to continue the level of services, previously provided to Danielle.

Neurological Evaluation:
February 19, 1999

Danielle Weathersby is now a nearly 4-year-old child with a diagnosis of Pervasive Developmental Disorder – Not Otherwise Specified, (PDD-NOS). As on her previous evaluation, Danielle has continued to make excellent gains across the board, most especially in social skills and language, but also in her pretend play. Motorically she continues to make good progress and toilet training is also evolving. Despite her good gains though, Danielle is showing some difficulties with inconsistent performance, limited expressive language, and the need for assistance, specifically in large groups.

Neurological Evaluation:
September 30, 1999

Danielle Weathersby is a 4-1/2-year-old girl, currently carrying a diagnosis of Pervasive Developmental Disorder – Not Otherwise Specified, (PDD-NOS). Danielle has continued to make exceptional progress not only demonstrated here in the office, but this assessment also includes the reports of her teacher and her therapists. Motorically, she now appears to be much more functional and is willing to risk challenging situations. Socially and language wise, she is also approaching other children, although her ability to expand on her language and to have multiple conversational exchanges remains slightly weak. Cognitively, Danielle appears to be at least equal to her peers and perhaps even a bit more advanced.

Neurological Evaluation:
March 23, 2000

Danielle Weathersby is now a 5-year-old child. She has continued to make exceptional progress, not only demonstrated by her presence here in the office, but also verified by the classroom teachers, therapists, and parents. Motorically she looks wonderful and also appears to be more socially on target and appropriate as well as quite competent language-wise. Occasionally there remains some remnants of language disabilities to the extent that when asked a question, she tends to turn away in an attempt to answer it. She does not always answer the question in a demand situation. It is difficult to know how much of this relates to being 5 years old and how much of this relates to her underlying diagnosis. Certainly, both may be at play here. Nonetheless, Danielle will require ongoing monitoring in regard to potential language problems.

Neurological Evaluation:
February 1, 2001

Danielle Weathersby is now a nearly 6-year-old child, who has been carrying a diagnosis of PDD-NOS. Danielle has made incredible progress over the past several years and at the present time no longer fulfills the criteria for Pervasive Developmental Disorder in any category. Although it might be too soon to tell whether or not her previous symptoms will have any impact on her ability to achieve academically without any difficulty, the signs so far indicate that she is a bright little girl who seems to be keeping up at this point!

Printed in the United States
By Bookmasters